DEAR READER,

Since 2015, I've worked from home. That home has been in India, Romania, the US, and Guatemala. Years earlier, I had a job where I stayed home one day a week to focus on a special project. Then there was the year I negotiated working from London while my colleagues were in California so I could stay with my partner through a graduate program. Remote work has been a part of my career for a long time. It's given me the **flexibility** to pursue interesting work and earn an income as my life changes and grows.

What got me interested in remote work as a subject, however, was research showing how much more **productive** people can be when they opt in to it. I started interviewing founders of all-remote organizations and watched their businesses and practices develop. I wrote about new software designed to support remote setups. In the bigger picture, I saw a movement that's changing how people work and live for the better.

It isn't all rosy. Remote work certainly has its problems. But I hope through this book you'll see what remote work can be when it's **done right**.

Sincerely,
Jill Duffy

WELCOME TO THE EVERYTHING® SERIES!

These handy, accessible books give you all you need to tackle a difficult project, gain a new hobby, comprehend a fascinating topic, prepare for an exam, or even brush up on something you learned back in school but have since forgotten.

You can choose to read an Everything® book from cover to cover or just pick out the information you want from our four useful boxes: Questions, Facts, Alerts, and Essentials. We give you everything you need to know on the subject, but throw in a lot of fun stuff along the way too.

QUESTION
Answers to common questions.

FACT
Important snippets of information.

ALERT
Urgent warnings.

ESSENTIAL
Quick handy tips.

We now have more than 600 Everything® books in print, spanning such wide-ranging categories as cooking, health, parenting, personal finance, wedding planning, word puzzles, and so much more. When you're done reading them all, you can finally say you know Everything®!

PUBLISHER Karen Cooper
MANAGING EDITOR Lisa Laing
COPY CHIEF Casey Ebert
PRODUCTION EDITOR Jo-Anne Duhamel
ACQUISITIONS EDITOR Rachael Thatcher
DEVELOPMENT EDITOR Peter Archer
EVERYTHING® SERIES COVER DESIGNER Erin Alexander

The Ultimate Resource for Remote Employees, Hybrid Workers, and Digital Nomads

THE **EVERYTHING**® GUIDE TO

REMOTE WORK

YOUR STEP-BY-STEP GUIDE TO:
- Working and thriving in a digital environment
- Avoiding distractions and optimizing productivity
- Maintaining a work-life balance
- Mastering the art of digital communication
- Continuing growth as an employee

JILL DUFFY

Adams Media

New York London Toronto Sydney New Delhi

Adams Media
An Imprint of Simon & Schuster, Inc.
100 Technology Center Drive
Stoughton, Massachusetts 02072

An Everything® Series Book.

Everything® and everything.com® are registered trademarks of Simon & Schuster, Inc.

First Adams Media trade paperback edition January 2022

ADAMS MEDIA and colophon are trademarks of Simon & Schuster.

For information about special discounts for bulk purchases, please contact Simon & Schuster Special Sales at 1-866-506-1949 or business@simonandschuster.com.

The Simon & Schuster Speakers Bureau can bring authors to your live event. For more information or to book an event contact the Simon & Schuster Speakers Bureau at 1-866-248-3049 or visit our website at www.simonspeakers.com.

Interior design by Alaya Howard
Interior images © 123RF/Vladimir Yudin, Stefan Amer, Ivan Ryabokon, Amornism

Manufactured in the United States of America

1 2021

Library of Congress Cataloging-in-Publication Data
Names: Duffy, Jill, author.
Title: The everything® guide to remote work / Jill Duffy.
Description: Stoughton, Massachusetts: Adams Media, 2022. | Series: Everything® | Includes bibliographical references and index.
Identifiers: LCCN 2021043850 | ISBN 9781507217863 (pb) | ISBN 9781507217870 (ebook)
Subjects: LCSH: Telecommuting. | Virtual work teams.
Classification: LCC HD2336.3 .D84 2022 | DDC 331.25/68--dc23/eng/20211006
LC record available at https://lccn.loc.gov/2021043850

ISBN 978-1-5072-1786-3
ISBN 978-1-5072-1787-0 (ebook)

CONTENTS

ACKNOWLEDGMENTS

To the team at Simon & Schuster and Adams Media who made this work possible, thank you. This book would have been lacking in ideas and detail if not for conversations with (in alphabetical order): web entrepreneur Dave Dean; Nick Francis of Help Scout; Nicole Miller at Buffer; Erinique Owens at Zapier; Carole Rosenblat of the Drop Me Anywhere project and blog; Amir Salihefendic of Doist; Mariano Suarez-Battan of MURAL; and all the unsung people in PR who helped coordinate conversations.

Many thanks also go to several insightful people for their input and conversations well before this book ever took shape, including David Allen of Getting Things Done; Jason Fried of Basecamp; Professor Emeritus Alan Hedge, now retired from Cornell University; and Professor Dr. Till Roenneberg at Ludwig-Maximilians-University Munich. Finally, a round of acknowledgment to all the colleagues, coworkers, and clients who have seen the remote work light and walked right on into it.

INTRODUCTION

In March 2020, millions of workers went home from work and were told not to come back. Instead, they were instructed to do their jobs from somewhere else. No one knew how long it would last. Nearly everyone had questions. The onset of the COVID-19 pandemic meant that thousands of businesses converted overnight to remote work, though only a tiny fraction of them were experienced at it. Yet those relatively few people and organizations have paved the way for a future of remote work. They're the ones who can teach you how to do it.

When remote work is done right, it's one of the most rewarding ways of working. Doing it right is the key. And in *The Everything® Guide to Remote Work*, you'll find the skills and information you need to fit into this new world. You'll learn:

- Whether your job can be performed remotely, in part or in its entirety
- How to set up a space for remote work and how to establish your work hours
- The best ways to organize conference calls with your colleagues
- Tips for dealing with in-home distractions
- Ways to track and share your on-the-job progress

With this knowledge, you'll be able to work remotely better, happier, and more effectively. And the benefits of remote work extend beyond the time you spend with your employer. When you work for an organization that truly embraces remote work and all the practices that make it possible, you have greater autonomy over your time, more flexibility in how you live and work, and options for new life experiences that may not have been possible before. You can spend more time with your family, adopt a pet and be around to bond with it, or travel the world while working. Having a remote job opens up many possibilities.

For you to be successful in a remote job, you have to know what makes remote work, well, *work* and some of the common problems that come up so you can navigate them and perhaps even resolve them. You should also be aware of all the ways you, as an individual, have to look out for and care for yourself to be happy, fulfilled, and rewarded as a remote worker.

In the world of remote work, "remote-first" describes organizations that build their businesses purposefully to support decentralized ways of working. The goal is to come up with policies, procedures, and a culture that support remote work and remote workers. The beauty of the remote-first framework is it still allows for in-person employees to communicate, collaborate, and participate as well.

The remote-first approach values output over hours; it believes in worker autonomy and strives for overcommunication. It says work can be done asynchronously much of the time. And the time a team does spend synchronously together should be used with maximum efficiency.

Granted, not all remote organizations live these values to the fullest, and remote work certainly has its pain points. No one said it was going to be perfect. But as companies become more experienced in managing a largely remote workforce, they're learning that taking a remote-first approach is a much better way to do business.

The more you know about remote work, the better prepared you are to succeed. It benefits you to learn about all the possible configurations that remote work can have. You should know about the best practices remote-first companies have already figured out that make their businesses run effectively and productively. You should learn about everything you can do to get the most out of working in a remote role so that it's a fulfilling experience, while also watching out for common pitfalls. You deserve to have a wealth of ideas for how to grow and develop your career as a remote worker, whether you're employed or independent. You'll find all that information and more ahead.

CHAPTER 1

Defining Remote Work

Remote work isn't one thing. It's a way of working. It's a lifestyle. It's a movement. It's the new direction for business. Remote work is about more than deciding where you want to be while you get your job done. For remote work to *work*, organizations and employees have to embrace a new way of operating. Taking an existing business, moving everything online, and hoping for the best is not the route to success. All the processes of a business and even the organizational culture must be rethought within this new framework.

Remote Work Takes Many Shapes

There's no one way to work remotely. It takes many shapes depending on the worker, the organization, the type of work being done, and other factors.

At the core of remote work is the idea of working somewhere other than a designated location shared with other workers. While it can be synonymous with working from home, it doesn't have to be.

Solo entrepreneurs working in a home office, for example, could be considered remote workers, even though they aren't technically "remote from" another location. The same goes for full-time employees of a company that has no headquarters or offices (an all-remote organization), where everyone works from a location that they choose. People who spend some time working in an office and some time working from a location of their choosing are also considered remote workers, even if they call it "flexwork" or "hybrid."

ESSENTIAL

The word "organization" refers to a variety of business types, including not only private companies but also nonprofit organizations, government agencies, microbusinesses, and solo entrepreneurs (such as freelancers and contractors), among others. Remote work is not limited to the private sector, and the term "organization" is intended to reflect that.

In some fields, people still refer to remote work as "telework," regardless of whether they use telephones to do their jobs. In a few cases, you might even still hear the term "cottage industry."

Whatever you call it, remote work starts with a job or series of tasks that are not location-dependent. Since you can do them practically anywhere, you get to choose where you work. From there, remote work is about building processes and an organizational culture that help remote workers get their jobs done as effectively as possible.

Full-Time Remote

A full-time remote worker is someone who works from a location of their choosing nearly all the time. The location could be their home, but it might also be a coworking space, a library, a coffee shop, or even a temporary residence, like a short-term rental or vacation home. Because full-time remote workers choose where they work, they may change the location day by day based on needs and preferences. For example, if there's a lot of loud construction happening near their home when they need to concentrate or hold virtual meetings, a full-time remote worker might work from a different location until it's over.

> **ESSENTIAL**
>
> It's impossible to talk about remote work today without acknowledging the COVID-19 pandemic. In 2020, remote work became mandatory for many people overnight. They didn't opt in to it, and their employers didn't necessarily adapt to be compatible with remote work. If your only experience working remotely was during the global pandemic, you may not know how good it can be to work remotely when there's not an international emergency.

Full-time remote workers usually have colleagues, coworkers, or clients with whom they communicate and collaborate virtually. In some cases, like a full-time vlogger who does all their own production, they may work entirely independently.

Part-Time Remote or Hybrid

A part-time remote or hybrid-remote worker divides their time between a central work location and locations of their choosing. This setup is more common in organizations that still believe a central location is important to doing business.

The reasons for being a part-time remote worker vary. Some executives insist that in-person collaboration is still the best way to achieve business goals. Another reason is that certain tasks must be performed in person. IT personnel might have to perform maintenance work or upgrades on physical equipment from time to time. Organizations that have high-security protocols may not allow employees to access some information from a remote location, requiring them to be present in a secure location to conduct some of their business.

All-Remote Organizations

In an all-remote organization, every employee works from a location that they choose, and the organization doesn't have a headquarters location or any offices. All-remote companies of any real size are still somewhat rare, though they do exist and their numbers are slowly growing. It's much more common to find solo entrepreneurs and microbusinesses that fall into the all-remote category than large businesses.

> **FACT**
>
> Although all-remote organizations don't have offices, they may be required to have an address on file in the US, depending on how they legally register. The address could be a residence, a small rented space, or some other location. So when you see an address for an all-remote company, it doesn't necessarily mean they have an office there.

When an all-remote company has more than a handful of employees, it often makes an effort once or twice a year to bring employees together physically for a retreat or conference. In other words, remote employees may have opportunities to interact with their colleagues face-to-face on occasion.

Remote-First Organizations

Remote-first organizations are businesses that embrace remote work culture and flexibility but do not operate fully remotely 100 percent of the time. Usually, they have at least one physical location designated for working, but who uses those locations and how often varies.

A remote-first organization may allow the majority of its employees to work remotely full-time while requiring a designated team to work from an office. Or it might allow employees to opt in to working either from the central location or remotely. Or the office location could be used ad hoc. The variations on how to run a remote-first organization are endless. The key feature, however, is that remote-first organizations support remote work to a much greater extent than traditional office-based businesses. They typically build awareness and best practices about remote work into their organizational culture. Additionally, remote-first organizations usually start out with a remote-first mindset, rather than growing first as a traditional business and later converting.

Hybrid or Flexible Organizations

Hybrid or flexible organizations typically start out as traditional, location-based businesses and grow to accept remote work to some extent. The majority of organizations that participate in remote work have a hybrid or flexible approach.

ALERT

It's tempting to call nonremote jobs "office jobs," but there are plenty of shared work sites that aren't offices. The way to best capture the great variety of workplaces used by multiple people is to call them "location-dependent" or "location-based." It may sound clunky and awkward at first, but it's the clearest and most accurate description.

Hybrid or flexible organizations usually have rules and allowances for remote work. For example, they may grant employees the option to work remotely 100 percent of the time on a case-by-case basis. A highly valued twenty-year veteran employee who requests to work remotely to support a partner's need to relocate might get the go-ahead, while a newly hired entry-level staffer may be required to work on premises. Sometimes employees negotiate the ability to work remotely either flexibly or permanently as part of their contract.

Having a flexible remote approach has additional benefits for the business. When employees are set up to work remotely at the drop of a hat, organizations have business continuity built into them. During a natural disaster when travel may not be safe, for example, businesses can continue running because the employees are already set up to work remotely.

It's also possible for an organization to transition into a hybrid or flexible setup to accommodate a crisis. During the COVID-19 pandemic, some organizations required select staff members to be at a business location for at least part of their work time. For example, a few team members might have to perform maintenance and upkeep on critical infrastructure, such as servers, or they might have to go to a secure location to perform some specific job function. Many of those groups created an A/B schedule. Everyone on Team A goes to the office Monday and Wednesday, and Team B goes in on Tuesday and Thursday. That way, if someone from Team A gets sick, only Team A has to quarantine, allowing Team B to continue in-office work.

Not All Jobs Can Be Remote

While we've seen a dramatic increase in remote work, not all jobs can be done successfully from a remote location. At the same time, don't be too quick to assume there are no opportunities in a particular field just because you can think of a few examples of when remote work isn't possible.

Examples of Work That Cannot Be Remote

It's easy to think of a few examples of work that cannot be done remotely: food service, agriculture, transportation, manufacturing, law enforcement, lab-based sciences, cosmetology, and so forth. Some work must be done at a specific location or in person.

High-security jobs often can't be remote either. Think of all the work done at the Pentagon or Central Intelligence Agency that absolutely should not be conducted over someone's home Wi-Fi or telephone line. In a crisis, however, these organizations might be able to institute an A/B schedule, as described previously.

In that sense, it's important to think about specific jobs or tasks, rather than people or industries, that can or can't be done remotely. This point is especially important for young people as they consider their future careers as well as anyone considering changing careers. Don't rule out entire industries just because you assume they don't offer remote jobs.

Don't Write Off Entire Industries

Take healthcare, for example. There are roles within healthcare that require a human being to show up and provide hands-on care. An example is a medical imaging technician. Maybe one day self-service mammograms will be the norm, but we're not there yet. Once a technician captures medical images, however, those images are often sent to a cottage industry of radiologists who read and analyze them from home offices. There are indeed remote jobs in unexpected places.

> **FACT**
>
> According to the Centers for Disease Control and Prevention, telehealth visits increased 154 percent during the last week of March 2020 as compared with the same week in 2019. The sharp increase is attributed to COVID-19, but there may be an unexpected benefit: It's created more opportunities for remote work in healthcare, which may last well beyond the pandemic.

More generally speaking, telehealth (or "telemedicine" as it's sometimes called) has grown slowly over several decades, and then increased dramatically in 2020. As more patients are willing to try telemedicine, more opportunities are created for remote roles in the healthcare industry.

Roles That Benefit from In-Person Experiences

Finally, there are job roles that benefit from being done in person either because they're more successful that way or they're *perceived* as being more successful that way.

A couple of roles that get lumped into this latter category include salespeople and company executives, especially entrepreneurs while they are raising capital for their organizations. A long-held belief still permeates the business world that these people need face-to-face contact with others to have the greatest chances of success. Yet not every aspect of these jobs needs to be done in person.

There may be data to back up the claim that founders should meet in person with potential investors and that salespeople have a better chance of winning over customers when they can smile and charm them in real life. But that still leaves a lot of lead tracking, data entry, number crunching, and report building that can be done from anywhere.

Working Remotely As an Employee

As previously mentioned, remote work takes many forms. When you're a full-time employee of an organization, there are any number of remote work configurations you might find yourself in. You might work with a team or an entire organization where everyone is remote. You could be the lone full-time remote person while everyone else goes to a common location each day. It could be that you and a few others work remotely on a flexible basis. You might be asked to work remotely, or you might request to do it.

When you're hired as an employee as opposed to being an independent worker, you enjoy unique privileges but also face unique challenges related to remote work.

Remote Work Language in a Policy or Agreement

If you are a full-time employee of an organization, you should have a work agreement of some kind as well as some organizational policies that you probably signed when accepting the job or within the first few days after joining the team. Within that paperwork, you should expect to see some language related to remote work. How much detail may depend on how frequently you'll be working remotely.

For example, a flexible remote work agreement may require nothing more than a security form to acknowledge a few IT-related security protocols. If you're 100 percent remote, you should expect (or demand) a lot more detail, such as allowances for equipment and furniture, loan agreements for any equipment provided to you (including whether you'll need to return it), and so on.

Limitations and Requirements of the Employer

Full-time employees who work remotely should also expect to see some limitations or requirements in their remote work arrangement by the employer. These requirements might include hours when you must be available for meetings, which is common for teams distributed across many time zones. The requirements may also include expectations for business travel.

By requiring a few common hours, organizations guarantee that they can schedule mandatory meetings when all employees should be able to attend. They can also send a highly important message at a time when all employees will receive it at the same time. You don't want to be the sole employee working in Hawaii who learns about a major change to the organization six hours later than everyone else.

Working Remotely As a Contractor

Contractors are independent workers hired by an organization to perform a specific role or job function. Contractors working remotely usually have more flexibility than employees of an organization because, legally speaking, in the US at least, they are able to determine their own hours. That's part of the definition of a contractor.

Because contractors are not employees, they don't get the same protections or benefits offered to employees. In some remote work arrangements, especially those that involve a client in one jurisdiction and a contractor in another (for example, a client in the US and a contract worker in Vietnam), the contractor needs to be careful that all their rights are upheld and that they aren't expected to function exactly the same as a full-time employee. This can be a tricky situation because it's up to the contractor to figure out which country's laws protect them and how.

Contractors also may have to play by some of the client's rules of working remotely in order to keep the relationship happy.

Working Remotely As a Solo Entrepreneur

Solo entrepreneurs are people who run their own businesses but work alone. They typically have the most freedom to set their hours, move from place to place as they like, and decide which projects and work they want to accept. It may sound like a glorious life, but solo entrepreneurs usually have to hustle hard to make ends meet. Some examples of solo entrepreneurs include freelance writers and photographers, lawyers who are not attached to a firm, and psychologists with their own practice.

What's "remote" about a solo entrepreneur's work? These types of workers often work from a home office or rented space; they're remote from their clients, customers, or patients. Because they don't work in a location-dependent shared workspace, they are included under the larger umbrella of remote workers.

Pros and Cons of Remote Work

Having a remote work lifestyle comes with a lot of benefits as well as a few potential problems and challenges. What those challenges are depends on what kind of person you are and what kind of lifestyle you lead. For example, you might find working at home alone deeply rewarding for all the silence and privacy it provides, allowing you to focus more intensely on difficult tasks. Another person might find that solitude lonely and isolating. Each person's experience also varies based on other aspects of their personal life:

- Do you have small children who must be cared for?
- Are you a primary caregiver for an elderly relative?
- Are there restrictions on the office space you use?

You also don't have much control over the speed of the Internet service available where you live or whether the city has decided to undertake a three-month roadwork project right below your bedroom window.

With a few strategies and tools, it's possible to overcome a lot of the potential challenges of working remotely and bask in the advantages.

Increased Flexibility

Flexibility is one of the greatest benefits of working remotely. By and large, remote workers have increased flexibility with their time, location, and comfort as compared to location-dependent workers.

FLEXIBILITY WITH TIME

Flexibility with time means you have greater independence in deciding the best hours to get work done, whereas location-based workers are much more likely to be given specified working hours. Some remote jobs may still have time requirements, but generally speaking, the remote work movement values *getting work done well* over putting in *these specific hours* per day. If you like to work on hard tasks that require a lot of focus at 6:00 a.m. and take off for two hours in the middle of the day to attend a yoga class, a remote job may let you live that lifestyle. Some remote workers prefer to keep more regular hours, like 8:30 a.m. to 5:00 p.m. Having flexibility means you can set hours for yourself if you choose and break away from them when you need to.

There can be a downside to having flexibility with time. Some people find it harder to have the self-discipline to complete tasks and projects without set hours. Learning a few strategies for overcoming this challenge can help—more on that a little later.

FLEXIBILITY IN LOCATION

Flexibility in location is another wonderful perk of working remotely. Remote workers often have a few locations where they work, such as a dedicated home office, a seat at the kitchen table when they need a change of scenery, or a favorite café or library if they want to get out of the house. Not everyone takes well to using their home as their primary work location, however. Coworking spaces and flexible office rentals, including some you can rent by the hour, give you more options.

Another benefit of location flexibility is the freedom to travel. Think of all the calculations that go into taking vacation when you work at a location-dependent job. You have to figure out when your last day at work will be, book your trip according to your work schedule, get approval for the exact dates you'll be away, and so forth. With a remote job that offers time flexibility, you're much less tied to schedules and permissions when booking flights or choosing dates to be on the road. For example, you can fly to a destination on the least expensive day, work the following day or two, and officially kick off your vacation after that. Or maybe you've always wanted "to spend more time in a particular location. With a remote job, you can potentially spend a month or two in a short-term rental in your dream location, all while working as needed.

FLEXIBILITY IN COMFORT

Flexibility in comfort plays out in many ways—clothing, lighting, ambient noise—but a favorite example is the thermostat. Who hasn't felt too cold or hot at work while everyone else seems perfectly fine? When you work remotely, especially at home, you get to make all the decisions about what makes you most comfortable. Crack a window for some fresh air, put on your favorite fuzzy slippers, light a candle, or do whatever you like to make your work environment as pleasant as it can be.

Lack of Boundaries Between Home and Work

Related to flexibility is the matter of not having many boundaries between home and work when working remotely. When does the workday start and end? Should you sweep your kitchen floors on your lunch break? These are the kinds of questions that come up when you live and work in the same place.

The lack of boundaries can be a pro, a con, or both. Parents of young children, for example, might relish the opportunity to feed their kids lunch everyday while also cursing their remote work life at every temper tantrum. The same mixed emotions can occur with other family members and even pets. It's a joy to work all day with a little dog at your feet until she's insistent on taking a walk and you're still trying to finish an assignment.

When comparing location-dependent work and remote work, it's easy to assume that location-dependent work has firm and clear boundaries that separate work and personal life perfectly. Since the early 2000s, that really hasn't been the case, though. With the rise of email and team messaging apps like Slack, those lines have blurred quite a bit. Consider all the full-time employees with traditional location-dependent jobs who check email on nights, weekends, or vacations. Don't get too caught up comparing remote and location-based work. Both have their advantages and disadvantages.

No Commute

There's no commuting when you work from home. Even for remote workers who choose to travel to a coworking space or other location, they ultimately choose the location and therefore have agency over their commute. For people changing from a location-dependent job to remote work, getting rid of a commute means they get time back in their day.

While data shows that, for the most part, people do not enjoy commuting to an office, a commute can provide a time and space to separate work life from personal life. A half-hour train ride or drive every day might be the time when you decompress from work and leave it all behind before arriving home. Remote work doesn't have that kind of decompression time naturally built into the rhythm of the day.

There is another potential negative effect of not having to commute if you formerly traveled to work by walking (including walking in combination with taking transport), running, or cycling: You may get less physical activity when the need to commute is removed. That said, as a remote worker, you could certainly use the time you gain back from not having to commute as exercise time.

More Privacy (and Isolation)

Not being in a shared workspace means you have a lot more privacy. This is a real benefit for anyone who has had to endure working in an open-office plan, where there are no doors, walls, or cubicle partitions to save you from being seen, heard, or interrupted at any moment by anyone else in the shared space.

That's not to say that all home office environments are devoid of distractions, interruptions, and other people. Certainly, some remote workers have less privacy than others, depending on who else shares their home or workspace.

The dark side of having more privacy is when there's too much of it and you feel isolated or lonely. Many organizations often try to ease these feelings by offering optional social activities and online spaces where coworkers can develop a stronger connection to one another.

Some people cope with the isolation of remote work well by spending more free time (lunch breaks and time not spent commuting) with friends and family. Others struggle with isolation, and some even leave a remote work position to return to in-person work for the social connection it offers.

FACT

While feelings of isolation and disconnection are known problems in remote work, they're significantly less for workers who have prior experience working remotely, according to the Pew Research Center. It could be because experienced workers stay with organizations that know how to combat isolation or that people who feel the most isolation tend to leave remote work jobs.

Decreased Costs

The costs associated with working remotely are different from the costs of working at a location-dependent job. Whether you end up on top depends on your circumstances, although often people who switch from location-based work to remote work spend less in a few categories.

Not having to commute usually puts a little cash back in remote workers' pockets. People also save money when they shift away from the pricey restaurants, takeout spots, and delivery services that can be popular in location-dependent jobs in favor of eating from a well-stocked fridge and pantry at home. And long-term remote workers usually find that over the years, they don't spend nearly as much money on business attire as their location-dependent counterparts.

Increased Costs

One spending category where remote workers may have to sink a little more money is Internet service. Typically, remote workers are responsible for paying their own Internet bills, even in all-remote companies. Some companies might provide a monthly stipend to offset the cost, but it's almost always stipulated in the work agreement that employees will stay connected. Therefore, it's important to invest in a reliable, high-speed connection.

Depending on the type of remote worker—full-time employed, hybrid-remote worker, independent contractor, etc.—costs can go up for home office equipment and furniture. Your employer may provide an allowance for home office supplies, although it won't necessarily cover everything you need to be comfortable. Independent freelancers and contractors may be able to deduct some of these expenses from their taxable income, so keep track of what you spend and consult an accountant.

Maintaining a Proactive Attitude

Remote workers, regardless of whether they're full-time employees or independent workers, must develop and maintain a proactive attitude to be successful in a remote position. When they work separately from their boss, peers, IT support team, and other colleagues, it's hard for others to know when they need help. Remote workers must learn how to speak up for themselves, voice concerns, and be persistent when troubleshooting problems instead of sitting around and waiting for someone else to notice what they need.

Maintaining a proactive attitude comes easily to some and is a real pain point for others. It also gets harder for everyone when work is tough and morale is low. Being your own advocate seems easy in the abstract, but it's hard to do when you're busy solving problems at work and feeling the stress of trying to maintain a healthy balance between your work time and personal life. It does get easier with time, practice, and a few strategies (covered later), however.

Is Remote Work Right for You?

Before you opt in to a remote work arrangement or go looking for a job that's designated as remote, you ought to consider whether you're suited to a remote work lifestyle. The good news is that many people are suited to it, or at least they can be once they figure out how it works best for them. It can take a little trial and error to find what you like about remote work, what you don't like, and how to tweak your work arrangement, locations, office setup, and daily habits to make it as enjoyable as it can be.

QUESTION

What if I take a remote job and decide it's not for me?
Having a remote job is not a static situation. It's fluid and flexible, and how you feel about it will certainly change over time. Plus, there could be problems that have nothing to do with the fact that your job is remote. If something isn't working, identify what it is and make adjustments before calling it quits.

Care Responsibilities

Care responsibilities may also influence whether you want to work remotely or how often. Say, for example, you have an infant or toddler in the home. On the one hand, working remotely allows you to spend more time with them. On the other hand, some parents find that being around children pulls them away from their work, even if someone else is in the home to help provide childcare. The same can be said for other family members who require at-home care or supervision.

Having the option to work remotely and flexibly also allows people to provide elder care or patient care, or to simply spend more time with loved ones who are nearing the end of their lives.

Deciding whether or how often to work remotely when taking care responsibilities into account is not easy. If you're a location-based employee considering a remote work arrangement, discuss trying out remote work for a time to see how well it works before committing to it long term.

Home and Lifestyle

Beyond children and care responsibilities, there may be other issues related to your home and lifestyle that sway you toward or away from remote work. Remember, remote work opens up the possibility for more travel because where you choose to work is flexible. However, your life or lifestyle might have other circumstances that keep you close to home. If you live in a small apartment in a noisy building and can't travel easily, you might find that your work life is better when you go to a designated work location every day.

Self-Discipline and Accountability

Do you have the self-discipline and personal accountability to get your work done efficiently while working remotely? The only way to answer this question is to try working remotely, track your productivity, pay attention to what is and isn't working, make changes as you go, and decide for yourself.

You can also dive into your past. Have you had prior experience with remote work or something like it that might give you clues as to how well it will work out for you now or even what kinds of problems you might expect to encounter? If you've written a thesis, graded papers, tutored, or even completed a school or university project off campus, you might have done much of that work from a location of your choosing. How did it go? What was hard? How similar or different would those experiences be to doing your current (or future) remote job?

If you've established that remote work will suit your lifestyle and temperament, the next step is to find out what remote jobs are out there.

CHAPTER 2

Landing a Remote Job

If you're interested in finding an all-remote job or a position with an organization that emphasizes remote work (a remote-first organization), the good news is there are plenty of jobs available and more coming on the market all the time. The not-so-good news is they are highly competitive and tend to favor certain roles; engineering and programming are the most in demand. Still, there are positions in product management, HR, customer support, and other departments, and if you learn how to set yourself apart as a great remote candidate, you're sure to find something.

How and Where to Look for Remote Jobs

Remote jobs are highly competitive because there are no (or very few) geographical limits on who can apply. It's a boon to businesses that want to attract the best talent. For employers, there are a lot of considerations that come into play when looking for the right candidates, so don't get discouraged just because the pool of candidates is deep. You could have a leg up if you know what kinds of qualities organizations want to see when they consider whether a candidate will contribute positively to the organization and its remote culture.

When you're applying to jobs that are designated remote or are at remote-first organizations, the people looking at your job application and interviewing you want you to demonstrate your awareness of issues that are important to remote work culture. These issues include how you express yourself in written communication and your awareness of interacting with a globalized workforce, among others.

The hiring committee is also looking for signs that you understand its specific organization. If you can set yourself apart from other candidates in this regard by demonstrating your knowledge of the group and of remote work in general, you can stand out from other candidates.

There's an art not only to finding and getting an offer for a remote job, but also to negotiating its terms, preparing for your first day on the job, and getting to know a new team of remote coworkers.

Where to Look for Remote Jobs

Remote jobs are advertised just about anywhere that you would find general job advertisements. Some examples are job-related sites such as *LinkedIn*, *Indeed*, *Glassdoor*, and *The Muse*; specialty websites for job listings based on industry, such as *GitHub* for programmers and *Dribbble* for graphic designers; and local and national newspapers and their websites.

Another place to look for open positions is with online job boards that specialize in remote, flexible, and freelance opportunities. A few examples are *Remote.co*, *FlexJobs*, *Pangian*, and *We Work Remotely*.

As you learn more about organizations that are trendsetters in remote-first culture, you may find that you'd like to work for one of them, in which case you should go directly to their job listings page. Some of the organizations leading the way in the remote work movement are:

- Automattic
- Basecamp
- Buffer
- Doist
- Help Scout
- Hubstaff
- MURAL
- Wikimedia Foundation
- Zapier

If you're interested in working for a specific remote-first organization, be sure to learn as much as you can about what it does and how it operates. Subscribe to its blogs and follow its social media feeds. Doing so will show your interest in the organization and can help you hear about new job openings before they're listed elsewhere.

ESSENTIAL

A trend among remote-first organizations, especially those that are growing quickly, is to encourage enthusiastic job seekers to submit a resume and cover letter even if there isn't a current job opening. Occasionally, a team is so inspired by someone's qualifications and achievements that they create a position for them.

Ways to Search and Keywords

Some job search sites now include "Remote" as an option that you can enter in the location search field. That's a surefire way to find positions that will have an option to work remotely, but read the job ad carefully. Some employers may have a condition that permits the position to be remote only for a limited time before requiring in-person attendance. Or they might be looking for someone who can get to a central work location on short notice, so even though the job is remote, you need to live within a commutable distance.

Not all jobs that allow you to work remotely are designated as remote, so there are other keywords you may need to look for in the job ad to tip you off. Some of those terms are:

- Contract
- Cottage industry
- Flexible
- Freelance
- Home-based

- Partial remote
- Telecommuting
- Telework
- Virtual
- Work from home

Keep in mind that freelance, contract, and cottage industry jobs are different from full-time jobs that come with employee benefits. In these roles, you are your own boss, and the organization hires you to do specific work that you charge it for. Look at how long those positions will last too. Some freelance, contract, and cottage industry jobs are on a short-term basis.

Applying to Remote Jobs

Nearly all job applications start with written communication. Even if you have a connection with someone at an organization, the first step in making your application formal is to submit something in writing. Usually, these written materials consist of a resume (also called a "CV"), a cover letter, and sometimes an application. Depending on your field, you might have other materials to submit, too, such as code samples, writing clips, or a video reel. After you submit your application, someone from the team may contact you, and you'll communicate by email.

In the course of applying to any job, not just remote jobs, the hiring committee literally judges you based on your written communication. In remote work culture, however, communication is a really big deal. The focus on your ability to communicate during the application process is more intense. The hiring team wants to see not only that you communicate well, but also that you communicate well in the context of remote work. Here are some ways to show you have what they're looking for.

Write Clearly for Message and Tone

Since the hiring team is going to pay very close attention to your ability to communicate clearly, the need to be clear should speak for itself. Written communication in any business must be clear to avoid confusion. In remote work, however, it's heightened. Because remote workers can work from anywhere, people may be in different time zones or otherwise communicating asynchronously. If a message is unclear, it could take hours or days for someone to ask for clarification and get a response. Being clear from the start helps to prevent that. That's why hiring teams are looking for job candidates to demonstrate that they understand the need for clarity in written communication.

In addition to clarity in the message, job candidates also need to be clear in tone and show their awareness of a globalized workforce. Unless you know the hiring team personally, leave jokes, sarcasm, and complex analogies aside. Don't assume that you know what's funny or will make sense to people from other places, countries, or cultures. Avoid sports idioms; for example: "move the goalposts," "knock it out of the park," and "par for the course." Be clear and professional during all stages of a job application and interview. If you get the position, you can learn later on when humor and sarcasm are welcomed in the organization.

When being clear in tone, politeness and courtesy go a long way. It's impossible to know how every person who reads your words will interpret them. By defaulting to politeness, you minimize the chance that someone will misunderstand your meaning.

Be Concise

Another aspect of being clear and efficient in written communication is brevity. Before submitting any application materials or sending any email, imagine yourself as a busy recruiter scanning emails and resumes ten at a time. Short, declarative sentences are easy to read. Paragraphs of two or three sentences are easier to visually scan than longer ones. When key information is in a bulleted list or boldface, it jumps off the page.

When you are concise in your job application materials, you help the hiring team review and assess your viability as a candidate quickly. Additionally, you demonstrate that you know how to communicate effectively. Once again, such communication is important to a remote team because ineffective communication creates a lag and slows down progress.

Pick Up on Written Communication Cues

There's a really simple trick to figuring out how to communicate best with new people: Follow their cues. When applying to a new job at a remote-first organization, read the company's blog, sign up for its newsletter, follow its social media channels, and then pay attention to what the content in these materials says and how.

Do the same thing with emails when you start corresponding with someone from an organization. What words do they use to talk about their work and culture? How do they go about asking for availability for meetings?

Try to mirror their language, tone, and style without mimicking it. A good candidate is someone who can pick up on how the team operates and participate in the same way. If there's a word or phrase you don't understand, check whether the organization uses it elsewhere on its website or in other writing, and if you still can't figure it out, ask what it means before you start using it. The hiring team pays close attention to these things. Asking a question when you don't know something can show that you're honest and humble. It also demonstrates that you actively participate in making sure communication is clear.

Tailor Your Submission Materials

Every time you apply to a job, regardless of whether it's remote, you create a custom resume or CV, cover letter, and other submission materials. The purpose is to provide materials that show your relevant experience to the job, not an exhaustive list of every work experience and responsibility you've ever had.

For remote jobs, you need to take extra steps to further tailor your submission materials appropriately. Most important is to make sure your resume or CV meets requirements of the country or region where the organization is technically located or where it primarily does business. A hiring team in Singapore will have different expectations for what's on your resume than one in California. Some countries require personal details that would be downright inappropriate on a US resume, such as date of birth and marital status. Do some research and learn what's expected and appropriate for the country, culture, or region.

Another way to tailor your application materials is to mention experiences you've had working remotely or working with distributed teams. These mentions can be subtle rather than put in bold and made obvious. For example, if you worked partially remotely in a previous role, you might include "and remote" on the location line of that job on your resume. If you worked with a distributed team or coworkers who were full-time remote, sneak a reference to that detail into a bullet point outlining your specific achievements and experiences.

Tips for Interviewing

You've made it past the initial application screening, and someone from a remote-first organization wants to arrange an interview with you. Great! Just as you did in your written communication, use your interview process to demonstrate your awareness of issues that are relevant to remote work.

Scheduling Interviews

Remote teams are sensitive to time zones. When arranging for an interview, always provide your time zone, and give it in multiple ways to make it easy for people to understand! For example, "I'm in Honolulu, and the time zone is HST (UTC-10). That's three hours behind California right now. There's no daylight saving time here, though, so it'll change by an hour later in the year."

Even though people at remote-first organizations are sensitive to time zones, everyone screws it up at some point. Don't be ashamed to look up time zones, including your own, and verify the local time for you or someone else before a meeting or deadline.

A standard Internet search for "What time is it in…" goes a long way and will likely lead you to TimeandDate.com, Time.is, or 24TimeZones.com. All are useful sites and can compare what time and date it is where you are with a city that you specify. Calendar apps, including Google Calendar and Microsoft Outlook, have a function that lets you schedule an appointment using a different time zone and still see the appointment on your calendar in your local time zone.

When someone confirms a time and date for an interview, they may write it out with the time zone of the person or people who are interviewing you and your own time zone. Always double-check that they got it right. You don't want to miss a job interview due to someone else's error.

Case Study: Buffer's Time Zone Employee Map (Hosted on Timezone.io)

Buffer, a remote company that makes software and tools for social media management for businesses, has a publicly available employee time zone map at timezone.io/team/buffer. This map shows a handful of time zones listed horizontally across the top in order, starting with Portland, Oregon, and going across to Sydney, Australia. It also states the current local time for each time zone. Beneath are thumbnail profile pictures of most employees. Hovering over a picture reveals each person's name and their city. Buffer's employee time zone map is a really simple and beautiful example of an effective way to keep people aware of colleagues' time zones.

Preparing for Video and Phone Calls

Most job interviews at remote-first companies take place via video or audio call. If someone sends a meeting invite with instructions to join via a service that allows both video and audio, such as Zoom Meetings (often just shortened to Zoom) or Google Meet, assume you will use video and prepare yourself and your space to look professional.

ALERT

Never join a web conference link more than two or three minutes early for a job interview! Never test the link in advance either. The reason? Organizations sometimes reuse links. If you test the link before your scheduled call time, you risk unexpectedly crashing another meeting, and that looks really bad!

About ten minutes before the call, make sure you have the right software installed and check it for updates. To test your audio and video, use features included in the software settings rather than testing the link to join the call.

For a video call, try to use a headset and microphone if you have them because they reduce ambient noise. Tidy up everything in the camera's view. Dress appropriately as if you were going to an on-site interview; what's considered business professional attire varies by industry. Do your best to make sure your face is lighted and that you aren't backlit. You might have to turn your chair so your back isn't toward a window or lamp.

During the call, if multiple people have joined, pay attention to whether people mute their microphones when they're not speaking, and follow suit. Everyone has different ideas about when to mute, and the best thing you can do when you're new to a group is pay attention to their behavior for guidance.

Knowing the Right Questions to Ask

The single best thing you can do before interviewing with a remote-first organization is read everything you can find about the company, starting with its own website and blog. Remote-first companies operate on the premise that the most efficient way to disseminate information—to not only employees but also customers, clients, and potential job candidates—is to write it down and make it accessible. Therefore, a lot of remote-first groups publicly post their statement of purpose, values, policies, benefits package, and other information. Read it! It will answer a lot of questions you have.

ESSENTIAL

While many candidate screenings happen via video call, some organizations use bots instead of humans for them, thanks to a new industry of AI virtual interview services. Before accepting a virtual screening, ask the organization what software is used so that you can read up on how it judges your speech, body language, and performance. It'll help you prepare.

After you've read everything you can about the organization, you might still be left with some questions, which you can ask about in the interview. Here are some to consider.

"What is the organization's policy on business hours and flexibility?"

Ask if there are any required business hours when you will be expected to work. You might also ask if there are any regularly scheduled mandatory meetings, and, if so, when they are typically held.

"What is the organizational culture regarding flexible hours?"

Depending on the nature of the job and structure of the team, you might also ask if there will be times when the team anticipates intense workloads and working overtime. Asking these questions doesn't mean you'll be scared off by the answers. It means you're trying to develop clear expectations of when, how, and to what extent you need to be available to be successful at the job.

ALERT

In a remote job interview, be prepared to answer this question: "How do you know you can work effectively remotely?" It's okay if you don't have direct career experience. Talk about other kinds of work or responsibilities that you saw to completion without a boss over your shoulder, from writing a thesis to creating a podcast or game with friends remotely.

"Is transparency part of the organizational culture, and if so, how?"

While some teams believe their organizations are highly transparent, the best way for you to judge if it's true is to ask for clear examples. Does the organization make salaries or salary ranges available to all employees?

Does the organization share information on how it attracts a diverse candidate pool? Does it look critically at employee demographics, including how many women or people of color receive promotions or hold high-level positions? Is there a clear process for promotion? What kinds of information does the organization share with the media and the public?

You don't want to come off as challenging an organization on its transparency in a job interview, but it is a great opportunity to ask questions that you really want answered, especially when interviewing at organizations that purport to be highly transparent.

BUSINESS TRAVEL

"How often will this position require business travel, including for retreats and team meetings?"

Some remote organizations are passionate about holding all-hands retreats and in-person team meetings once or twice per year. Ask how often business travel will be expected of you, if you are offered the position. If you have personal or family circumstances that make traveling difficult or inconvenient, ask additional questions such as whether family members may accompany employees on business travel or whether there are other accommodations available for people who might need more flexibility.

You can ask these kinds of questions without giving too much away about your personal life by saying something like "How does the organization accommodate such and such?"

TIME OFF AND HOLIDAYS

"How does the organization approach time off and holidays?"

"What is the average number of days off employees take per year?"

Remote-first organizations often have employees who are located in different countries. Different countries observe different holidays and have different laws about paid time off (PTO) for employees. For that reason, it can be incredibly complicated to come up with a calculation for paid time off and holidays that will be fair to all employees. As a result, many remote organizations take a totally different approach, offering unlimited paid time off or a generous number of days off per year that aren't pegged to any particular holiday. For example, employees might get forty days off per year, and they can spread them out over local holidays, vacation time, and personal days as they see fit.

So-called unlimited PTO is never truly unlimited, and it can be a tricky benefit for employees to navigate. That's why it's in your interest, as a job candidate, to ask how many paid days off employees take on average per year. A good follow-up question is whether that number includes or excludes national holidays.

Case Study: How Doist Arrived at Its Forty Days PTO Policy

The all-remote company Doist has employees across the globe, and everyone gets forty days of paid time off per year to use as they please. CEO and founder Amir Salihefendic says his team came up with that policy as a way to encourage everyone in the organization to take sufficient time off and make it fair for everyone, regardless of their nationality.

Before it arrived at this policy, the company had tried offering a number of vacation days plus national holidays for whatever country each employee lived in. "The problem was when we looked at the stats, there was a huge difference in the number of national holidays in different countries. So some people were getting a lot more time off," Salihefendic says. As he and his company looked at the regulations in various countries and considered how they, as the employer, would comply with them, they decided the easiest solution would be to meet the most generous regulation and apply it to everyone. The resulting policy is in line with what the Nordic countries mandate for time off, and now everyone at Doist benefits from it.

Why didn't Doist instead offer an unlimited time-off policy, as many other tech companies do? According to Salihefendic, it's "one of the worst policies you can have." What happens is the leadership team doesn't tend to take time off, and when employees see their bosses always working, they feel that they shouldn't take time off. So instead, Salihefendic says everyone is encouraged to take all forty days, "and most people in the company do. We've been doing this for more than a decade now. Burnout and mental issues, they're huge problems for knowledge workers. You really need to combat them. It's really short-sighted to not take vacation."

TOOLS USED FOR COLLABORATING

"What software or tools does the team use to collaborate?"

By finding out what tools and methods people use to collaborate, you might get a sneak peek at how the team operates and how well it's going. If an interviewer answers this question with a few key apps, that's a sign they've worked out their kinks and are committed to using a primary set of tools. If the answer is a laundry list of apps, it could be a sign that the team is still developing its norms and processes—and that's okay. Some people like to be included in figuring out which systems work best for communicating and collaborating. Others prefer to enter a job after the trial and error needed to find the right tools has already been done.

Whatever the answer, you might want to watch some video tutorials of any tools an interviewer mentions that you're unfamiliar with.

Other Topics and Questions

The questions you'll want to ask in a job interview for a remote position will change depending on how much you learn from reading information that the organization makes public. As previously mentioned, it's very common for remote-first teams to make their benefits, policies, and style of working public on a website or blog.

Here are a few more questions you might ask in an interview if you don't find answers elsewhere:

- What equipment or budget do employees get to set up their workspaces?
- Are there allowances for coworking spaces?
- How does the team handle remote onboarding?
- What are some of the ways the organization celebrates successes and keeps morale high?
- Are there any social groups or activities for employees?

While you should ask plenty of questions related to the remote environment and benefits, don't forget to come up with questions that are specific to the position too! Those questions are more important and should take precedence over asking about the remote culture.

Negotiating Remote Work Benefits

In the final stages of any job interview (not just remote jobs), you and the employer may negotiate the salary. You might also negotiate your paid time off, such as how quickly it accrues and when you can take it, as well as other benefits.

ESSENTIAL

In all job interviews and negotiations, be mindful of the semantic difference between "the organization" and "you/your." For example, when negotiating a salary, it makes a huge difference to ask, "Is *the organization* able to offer 10 percent more?" rather than "Can *you* make it 10 percent more?" That small change in language makes negotiating less personal for the interviewer and interviewee. In remote jobs, sometimes paid time off isn't negotiable, especially when it is a flat and generous allowance to all employees, such as unlimited PTO or more than thirty days per year. There are other benefits and perks the company may offer, though, which you might be able to negotiate.

Learning and Education

Some remote teams have a budget for employee education and learning. If so, find out what it does and does not cover. If there's something you're eager to learn or continue learning, you might be able to negotiate a stipend or reimbursement for it. Think beyond programming classes and leadership development workshops.

You might be able to convince an employer that it's in their interest to support you as you study a language, learn a musical instrument, or subscribe to a generalized learning site, such as *MasterClass* or *LinkedIn Learning*. Research published in 2014 in the *Journal of Occupational and Organizational Psychology* showed that mastering a skill, even when it's unrelated to work, makes for better workers and increased productivity.

Discounted Gym Memberships or Equipment

In location-dependent work, employers sometimes offer a gym on-site, complimentary gym memberships, or a discount to a health and fitness club. Why shouldn't remote workers get a similar benefit?

Depending on where you live and what activities you like to do, you might be able to negotiate something that fits your lifestyle better than a gym membership. Would the employer be willing to provide a twice-yearly stipend to offset the costs of your rock climbing hobby or yoga classes, for example?

Other Perks and Expenses

You can negotiate other perks based on what the organization offers and what makes sense for you and your lifestyle. Food and beverage perks often come up. If an organization were running a location-based business, they'd probably offer employees coffee, tea, and maybe snacks. Remote employees might instead get discounts to subscription services for food and beverages.

If those perks and benefits don't work for you for whatever reason, ask if there's something else you can get instead that's of equal value. You'll have the best shot at negotiating these kinds of perks if you've already thought of what you want and come up with a rationale for why it makes sense. If the employer doesn't have to do much work to give you the benefit, they're more likely to say yes.

Successfully Navigating Remote Onboarding

Once you've accepted a job offer for a remote position, now what?

In the week or two leading up to the official start date of a new remote job, you will most likely be expected to do a little bit of work, such as receive and set up your equipment. The organization may ship supplies to you, such as a laptop and monitor. Or you may be asked to buy the primary equipment you'll need before your first day and then file an expense report for it later. You'll have to verify all the equipment works before day one. Most other work can wait for your first week on the job.

Save Some Work for Your First Week

Your colleagues may send you invitations to set up your email and join the software accounts they use to communicate and collaborate. You might receive dozens of links to resources, such as an employee handbook that you will have to read and sign and training videos you must watch. This is work you should save for your first week or two. Don't do it in advance; wait until you're getting paid for it. Plus, you might find that in the first few weeks, you need some busywork to fall back on.

Just because your team members send you lots of tasks and information in advance doesn't mean they expect you to complete it all right away. Remember, remote teams are often used to working asynchronously. New colleagues and managers may send you information at their convenience and expect that you'll review it at yours. Pace yourself.

Expect a Lot of Meetings at First

In your first week or two at a remote job, expect to be invited to a lot of meetings. People want to meet you. They may also want you to join meetings just so you can observe how things work and start to pick up on the state of projects.

This influx of meetings can be overwhelming, and it can be even more of a shock if you suddenly have no meetings on your calendar after the first two weeks. Again, pace yourself, and know that it's not unusual to be invited to an unusually high number of meetings when you're brand-new to a team.

If You Feel Abandoned

Sometimes in remote onboarding, your colleagues put so much effort into filling your first two or three days with activity that they don't plan for much after that. For you, the new employee, it's easy to feel inundated with meetings, reading assignments, and training videos, and then feel suddenly abandoned.

It's not unusual, so don't worry about it too much. Do ask for help, support, and instruction as needed. If you saved readings and training videos that people sent you before your first day, this is the time to go through them. You might even ask your manager or boss for a short daily check-in until you get your bearings. As much as everyone at a remote organization wants you to be able to work independently, no one expects you to operate in a silo or to know everything about the team and its work after only a few days on the job. Pace yourself. Have patience. Ask for help.

As you get to know the people on your team, you'll identify who can answer specific questions, give you assignments, and otherwise guide you into acclimating to the team.

Getting to Know Your Team

During the onboarding process, you'll get to know all the people on your team and many other people in the organization. It helps to have some designated people (three will do) to whom you can go with questions: your boss or manager, a coworker on your team or in your department, and a third person who works in a different department, if available. In very small organizations, it might not be necessary to have more than one or two people to help you out.

Your boss or manager should guide you into your work and the organization. Expect to have regular meetings and check-ins, even if it's just a message on a team messaging app once or twice a day to see how you're getting along.

The next person to ask for help is a direct coworker on your team, when possible. This person should be able to answer specific questions about your job and how to do it. You might not meet with this person on any kind of schedule, but you should feel comfortable asking, "How do I…?" about any of your day-to-day responsibilities.

The third person—and this is more common in larger organizations—is someone outside your immediate team who can answer questions about organizational culture and who's who. Think of them as an office sponsor. Some organizations pair new hires with a sponsor to help them learn about the organization from someone with a different perspective.

Aside from knowing whom to ask when you have questions, there are other ways to meet people in a remote organization. If there are team messaging channels for socializing and common interests, you'll be sure to hear about them. People will tell you if there's a book club, virtual happy hour events, and other online social groups. There could be occasional in-person meetups if several people live in the same region. Find out about these opportunities and even if they don't seem particularly interesting, join some of them to get a sense of what they have to offer. You might find that many months into your job you need more social connection from your coworkers. It's better to give these socializing opportunities a try early on and decide later if they're not a good fit for you.

Setting the Tone Early of Speaking Up Quickly

One of the most important things you can do in the first few days and weeks of working as a new hire at a remote-first company is speak up quickly when you need something.

Remote organizations rely on employees to speak up when they have a need, question, or problem. No one is going to stop by your desk, notice that your chair is broken, and order a new one for you. You have to be fully committed to asking for what you need when you need it.

When you're new to a remote organization, speaking up early sets the tone that you will do the same going forward. And you're not just setting the tone for your boss or manager; you're also creating the habit for yourself. If you don't ask for help the first time you need something, you may be hesitant to do it in the future, and then problems fester and questions go unanswered. No one wants that. So make a habit of addressing problems and asking questions promptly.

Successful remote employees speak up in all kinds of situations. That doesn't mean you should treat every little matter as if it's urgent. When you know what you need, decide the best way to express it, communicate the issue clearly and concisely, and then follow through in resolving it. It also helps to be solution-oriented from the get-go. In other words, if there's a problem and you have an idea for a solution, offer it from the start. Being proactive in this way shows that you're engaged.

CHAPTER 3

Setting Up to Work Remotely

Once you have a remote job, you'll want to set up some kind of workstation in your primary remote work location. When starting a new all-remote job, this phase can be exciting and fun. You get to create your own space and design it the way you want. It's worthwhile to put in some time and thought to make a nice space to work, regardless of whether you're remote full-time or only sometimes. Feeling happy and comfortable makes it easier to focus, and making your setup ergonomic prevents injuries too.

Making a Dedicated Space

When you get a new full-time remote job, you have to think about making a dedicated space to work, whether it's at home, in a coworking space, or elsewhere. If, however, you slowly ease into a remote work arrangement, such as a hybrid or flexible schedule, there might never be one single day when you realize you need to set up a proper workstation. If you don't work from home consistently, it's easy to shrug off the need for a good desk, chair, and everything else you need to work comfortably. Set aside a few hours to think about it, plan it, and eventually follow through on making a space for yourself.

It's an Ongoing Project

As you craft your workspace, remember that it can be an ongoing project. You don't have to unveil a new beautiful home office like you're on some interior design show. You can make changes at any time, and it doesn't have to be exactly what you want on the first day. Once you get into the rhythm of working, it might feel hard to change the position of your desk or invest the time and energy to find and buy the right office chair, but the option is always there. Don't ever feel stuck with what you have.

It's also possible to make small, temporary changes to alleviate problems until you find the time to address them more fully (for example, putting a pillow behind your back until you find a chair with great lumbar support).

FACT

In reviewing studies related to indoor office conditions, researcher Yousef Al Horr of the Gulf Organisation for Research & Development and several coauthors identified eight factors that contribute to employee happiness and well-being in a 2016 paper published in the journal *Building and Environment*. They are: indoor air quality and ventilation, thermal comfort, lighting, noise and acoustics, office layout, proximity to plants and nature, look and feel, and location and amenities. Keep them in mind when designing your workspace.

Choose More Than One Place to Work

The first step in creating a home office workspace is to choose two spaces. Why two? Sitting in the same chair hour after hour, staring at the same wall or out the same window gets tedious. Pick a primary space where you can work and where you'll set up a great workstation, plus at least one other space that you can use when you need a change. For example, your primary space might be at a desk and your secondary space the kitchen or dining room table or the couch. Give yourself options.

For your primary workspace, set it up to have everything you need. You don't want to be jumping up from your chair to find a charger, for example, when one of your devices is suddenly low on battery life. Put everything you need within reach to minimize distractions.

For your temporary spaces, you don't need to build them out in any way. Just make sure they have adequate lighting and electrical outlets.

Here's another tip that may sound silly or obvious but is important for making a nice workspace: Make sure to include storage. Use all the drawers, shelves, bookcases, and other storage at your disposal. People have a tendency to let clutter accumulate on their desk even when they have a near-empty drawer or cabinet literally beneath their desk. Think about using all the available space you have on hand for your needs.

Creating Spatial Boundaries

Psychology plays a big role in creating a workspace that works for you, especially when you do your job and live your life under the same roof. As you set up places to work, pay attention to any physical and spatial boundaries that already exist and that help you define where you work. Additionally, you can draw new boundaries to help you corral your work life into a defined area so that it doesn't bleed into your personal time when you don't want it to.

Creating boundaries gives you better control over managing your work and personal time. "Control" is the key word. In remote work, there may be times when you embrace and appreciate the flexibility to not have boundaries. But when you want or need some boundaries, it's best if they're already in place and established.

People who tend to be very compartmentalized may draw and use spatial boundaries without even thinking about it. If you aren't compartmentalized by nature, you might have to put in a little effort.

An Office with a Door Is a Treasure

Most home office workers' preferred setup is to have a dedicated room for work with a door to close. If your home has an office, spare bedroom, or another private space (a finished basement, a converted shed) that you can use as an office, treasure it for all it's worth. Nothing beats a room with a door to create a spatial boundary for where you work.

Not everyone has an extra room with a door to use as an office, of course. There are other ways to create spatial boundaries, however, to help you separate work life from personal life.

ALERT

When choosing a primary workspace in your home, make sure there are sufficient outlets before setting up any furniture or equipment. Depending on your power needs and the wiring of your home, you may need to spread out your equipment over multiple outlets so as not to overload them.

Choose Your Chair Wisely

When deciding where to work, try to choose workspaces that differ in some way from your leisure spaces. For example, if you sometimes plan to work at the kitchen table, sit in a different chair from the one you use when you eat meals.

You can do the same thing with living room furniture, reserving the sofa for leisure time, for example, and an armchair for work, or vice versa. These kinds of spatial boundaries may seem insignificant, but they help your brain separate work time from personal time. In the long term, those signals contribute to a healthy and positive lifestyle.

Use Two Different Computers, If Possible

Some remote workers find that keeping two different computers, one for work and one for personal use, helps them establish boundaries. By never opening personal websites for online shopping or social media on your work computer, you're less likely to be distracted when you're trying to work. Likewise, if you never load business email or team messaging apps on your personal laptop or desktop computer, you'll be less tempted to get sucked into work issues on your time off.

If you work for an organization that has high-security protocols, it makes a whole lot of sense to keep your personal digital life and electronics completely separate from the ones you use for work.

You don't actually have to own multiple computers to create this type of spatial boundary between work and personal life. Another way to achieve a similar result is to create two user accounts or profiles on one machine. That way, you can log out of your business account at the end of the workday and log in to your personal account, and all your activities will be kept separate.

Plan Time in Spaces Outside the Home

Another way to create spatial boundaries is to plan times when you will leave the home and work in a different location, such as a library, coworking space, café, or a friend's home. Pick places that you enjoy, and plan in advance what kinds of tasks you'll do there. A café might have too many noises and distractions for tasks that require high focus, so plan to answer emails while there instead. Or you might find that you tend to make great progress on difficult work when you're at a coworking space or library, where the mere presence of other people makes you feel more accountable to staying put and working diligently until a task is done.

The Magic of Headphones

Headphones, especially noise-canceling, over-ear sets, create a spatial boundary, too, albeit an acoustic one. Headphones can help you turn your audio awareness away from the surrounding environment, which helps some people focus. Whether you listen to music, white noise, podcasts, audiobooks, or nothing is entirely up to you.

In shared spaces, headphones signal to other people that you don't want to be disturbed, so they create a spatial boundary in that sense as well.

> **ESSENTIAL**
>
> Invest in a high-quality pair of headphones with a microphone that fit comfortably and make you happy. They come in handy for remote work all the time, such as for video calls, drowning out or quieting noise around you, and possibly for business travel.

How to Set Hours Without Giving Up Flexibility

Similar to spatial boundaries, time-based boundaries help remote workers manage when they work and don't work. The way to set time-based boundaries is to create a schedule.

Just as with spatial boundaries, there are moments when having flexibility with time-based boundaries is much more important than sticking to firm rules. During times when you feel you need a schedule, however, you have to already have one in place for it to work. If you follow a time-based schedule only a few days a month, that's not a schedule. That's a daily agenda.

To put it another way, most remote workers find it helps them to set a schedule and stick to it. That way, when they need rules for when to work and not work, they can default to it. When they need flexibility, they can break away from the schedule with no problem.

When you choose to start your workday can be up to you, or it may be mandated by your remote job. Some teams have a morning check-in, whether it's a web conference meeting or just a quick group chat on a team messaging app, to nudge everyone to start working around the same time. Other jobs are time dependent, such as a customer support role with fixed, assigned hours. Some organizations and teams allow people to have full autonomy over the hours they choose to work.

> **ALERT**
>
> Very rarely do remote workers have complete autonomy over when they work. Nearly everyone has a responsibility to a team, manager, boss, or client to communicate roughly when they plan to work or when they can be available for meetings. Even with all its flexibility, remote work usually requires at least some advance planning related to working hours.

If you have a lot of flexibility in deciding when to start work, come up with a planned schedule and communicate it to your boss, manager, team, clients, or whoever else needs to know. Your schedule doesn't have to be the same every day, and it might change over the course of a year too.

If you have children, for example, how does their schedule affect when you can start work? How will their school or your childcare routine change throughout the year, and how do those changes affect your availability? If you live somewhere with seasonal weather or where the sun rises at different times during the year, how do those factors influence the times when you feel awake, alert, and ready to focus? Maybe you have a fitness class or running club that you like to attend on Mondays and Wednesdays, and you'd like to shift your work hours on those days to start and end later.

To summarize, there are two highly important pieces to setting a remote work schedule. First, make some kind of decision about when you plan to work—even if it changes later, even if it's not the same every day, even if you occasionally break from it. Second, communicate that schedule to the people who need to know and update them when it changes.

Setting a schedule is bound up with creating a healthy balance between work life and personal life—more on that later.

Getting Started with New Routines

Very few people live by the clock alone. The time on the clock is merely a guide. What you *do* at various points in the day has a lot more meaning in setting the rhythm of life than the hour. That's why it's one thing to set a schedule and another to follow a schedule by creating a daily routine.

Routines are, well, routine. They are a series of habits. And habits are, well, habitual. People form habits without thinking much about them. So when you develop a new routine, what you're really doing is putting new habits in place.

Habits take time to stick. Be patient because your remote work schedule may not feel easy at first. With a couple of tricks, however, you can start off strong and in all likelihood feel better about it over time until it becomes second nature. You'll learn in greater detail how to finesse these routines in Chapter 9.

Starting Your Day

Anecdotally, many remote workers have an easier time starting their workday than ending it. The reason could be because remote workers communicate their intended schedule to their colleagues and therefore feel accountable to be online and available by a set time each day. (It might also have to do with a mandatory meeting or check-in each day at a prescribed time.)

A good way to kick off the start of a workday is to pick an existing habit that you do at around the same time you want to start work and then always sit down to work right after you do the action. For example, the existing habit might be making a cup of coffee, writing in a journal, brushing your teeth, or anything else that you already do habitually. Just start your workday right after you do it.

Ending Your Day

As mentioned, remote workers seem to have a much harder time stopping work on a schedule than starting. In location-based jobs, people leave work when the clock says so, or when other coworkers leave, or when they have an obligation, like picking up family members on time or meeting a trainer at a gym. If you're home with no pressing obligations, however, the clock might seem less powerful. Plus, there are no other coworkers leaving to signal to you that it's time to stop working.

Think instead of a signal you can use to mark the end of the workday. If you have a dog or dogs, they can be wonderful at nudging you to wrap up your work and take them out for a walk; they'll learn quickly what time to expect it too. You might also create an obligation, such as calling or meeting a friend, or going for a daily walk, run, or bicycle ride. Consider picking up a new hobby and using it as your signal to stop working for the day. Remember, when you don't have to commute, you have more time to do things you enjoy. So start a garden, sign up for language-learning classes, take up birding, or whatever interests you. Then schedule your activity at the time you want to end your workday.

ALERT

In figuring out how you can signal to your brain and body that the workday has ended, it helps tremendously to physically leave the place where you work. Going outside or even moving to a different room in your home makes it clear that you're transitioning away from work and into personal time.

Making Time for Breaks

"Don't forget to eat lunch." You might hear your remote colleagues and peers joke that they get so caught up in working that they inadvertently skip meals. Admittedly, some people have the opposite problem and don't regulate their meals well when they have a kitchen and pantry at their disposal all day. Either way, meal breaks and other breaks are essential to having a positive remote work routine.

Eating is not necessarily what's important. It's the breaks. To operate at your peak potential, you need regular, restorative breaks. One of the ways to get them is to plan for them and make them part of your routine.

Breaks don't have to be at exactly the same time every day, but just like the rest of your routine, you'll have a better chance of sticking to your routine and making the actions within your routine habitual if you aim for consistency most of the time.

Pick a window when you will take a long break, about an hour for full-time workers, and then take the full break. Don't shortchange yourself. Silence work-related notifications (as long as it makes sense for your role and whatever is happening) and consider stepping away from all screens while you recharge.

In addition, take several shorter breaks throughout the day. They might be planned, or they might occur every so many minutes.

Changing Positions

When setting up your remote workspaces, you picked at least two places to work. One is your primary remote workstation, and the others are for a change of scenery.

In your day-to-day routine, practice making use of alternative places. Literally change your location from time to time. It breaks up the monotony of the day and also forces you to move a little bit, which is good for circulation and health. Think of changing areas as part of your shorter breaks.

Going Outside and Dedicating Time for Activity

Giving up a commute when shifting from location-based work to remote work means you get back all that time you once spent going to and from a job site. It also might mean you no longer have a reason to go outside twice a day. Active commuters, meaning people who walk, cycle, or run to work, as well as those who walk in combination with taking public transport, might also suddenly find themselves getting less activity than when they commuted. As a result, many remote workers have to put in extra effort to make time to go outside and be active.

Exposure to natural sunlight helps regulate circadian rhythms. In other words, it helps your body sleep at night. Sunlight is beneficial even when it's very cloudy out or during hours when UV rays are less intense (although you still need adequate sun protection, even when the sun doesn't feel strong).

Physical activity is not only important to physical health; it also contributes to overall wellness, happiness, and productivity.

What Do You Need in Your Workspace?

Setting up and customizing a primary workspace takes time and is usually an ongoing process. You don't have to have a perfect setup from day one, but it certainly helps to have a vision of what you would like so that you know what you're working toward.

Some of the furniture and equipment in your workspace will be necessary. Then there are other items that might make the space more comfortable, enjoyable, or functional, depending on your preferences and type of work.

Ultimately, what you need depends on the work you do. Some people absolutely need a printer. Designers sometimes need a digital stylus and tablet. Many of the specifics vary based on your occupation.

> **QUESTION**
>
> **Can I write off the cost of work-from-home equipment on my taxes?**
> It depends. Self-employed people, including freelancers, usually can deduct qualified business expenses, which may include equipment, furniture, and even square footage used for work. Full-time employees might not. Track your expenses and consult an accountant or tax expert for advice.

Furniture

A primary workstation needs furniture, namely a chair and desk or table. If you work remotely only occasionally, you might find that the kitchen or dining room table and a chair works just fine. If you're a permanent remote worker, it makes a big difference to have an adjustable chair with a comfortable and supportive back, plus a desk or table that you dedicate as your workspace.

Devices, Peripherals, and Accessories

Next on the list of requirements is the equipment you need. In most cases, you'll have a desktop computer or a laptop, plus some peripherals and accessories for it, such as an external monitor, keyboard, keyboard tray, and mouse.

If you have a laptop and no monitor, you might also consider getting a laptop riser, sometimes called a laptop stand. It raises the laptop a few inches off the table to put the display at eye level. When you use a laptop riser, you must also add an external keyboard and mouse because you can't type on the built-in keyboard or use the trackpad effectively when it's in this configuration.

Other common equipment, peripherals, and accessories include a printer, surge protectors, chargers and cables, headphones with a microphone or a separate mic, a desk lamp, and a trash can and/or recycling bin.

QUESTION

Should I get a sit-stand desk to work from home?
You don't need one to work comfortably, especially if you have an ergonomic setup and take frequent breaks from sitting. It's fine to have one if you use it properly, but the recommended standing time is often much shorter than people assume: Cornell University's Ergonomics website (CUErgo) recommends as little as eight minutes at a time.

Comfort Items and Odds and Ends

Beyond the core equipment you need to get your job done, there are other comfort items and odds and ends that can make your workspace better.

A back cushion is the number one item in this category. Very few home office chairs are comfortable and supportive enough on their own. Back cushions run the gamut in style and price, although you don't have to pay a lot for one that gets the job done.

A footrest is another item that can make a workstation much more comfortable. Whether you need one depends on the height of your desk or table, the length of your legs, and the height of your chair. For good posture, your feet need to be flat and supported. If you can't achieve that without a footrest, get one.

You might want pens, pencils, markers, notebooks, and sticky notes on hand. Houseplants, framed photos, candles, and aromatic diffusers certainly can make a space nicer. Keeping a dustcloth on hand allows you to wipe off your screens and surfaces quickly and easily. Other items that may make you more comfortable and happier while you work include a throw blanket, fan or air conditioner, humidifier or dehumidifier, air purifier, shelves, a box of tissues, a bottle of hand lotion, and so forth.

ALERT

In almost all remote work agreements, the employee is responsible for maintaining Internet service and supplying the necessary equipment to use it, such as a modem and router. You may want to upgrade those devices when shifting to a remote-work lifestyle to ensure they're in tip-top shape.

Don't forget to decide whether you want to paint the walls or add some curtains or blinds. It's your workspace. Make it what you want it to be.

ESSENTIAL

When shopping for a back cushion, take into consideration the length of the seat on your chair. A very large cushion will push you forward and could leave you without enough support under your legs. If the seat is quite short to begin with, look for a thinner cushion, or consider getting a different chair.

Asking for What You Need (from an Employer)

Full-time remote employees, and possibly some hybrid or flexible remote employees, should expect their employer to pay for some of the cost of their home office. You'll find out what they cover when you interview for the position or, for organizations that are shifting to remote work, as they develop their policies.

The most basic equipment, such as computing hardware (computer, mouse, keyboard, and monitor), should be paid for by the employer. Some organizations supply these items directly. Others ask employees what kind of computer they want from a list of options or give them a price limit and let the employees put in a request. Some organizations may allow employees to buy the equipment themselves and submit an expense report for it. Typically, remote organizations have a policy stating how often they will upgrade computer equipment too.

ESSENTIAL

People with accessibility differences or disabilities may have other requirements for their furniture and equipment. Whatever you need to get your job done, make sure you have it, and if you're employed full-time, request that your employer pay for it.

Any software or subscriptions you need for your job should also be paid for by the employer. The same goes for hardware repairs.

Furniture may or may not be included, depending on the organization and where you're located. It's not unusual for organizations to provide a furniture budget to employees once every so many years or to approve one-off expenses as needed for a chair, desk, or other furniture.

An in-home ergonomics consultation is one perk some remote companies offer, although whether you can claim the benefit may depend on where you live and how easy it is to find a qualified consultant in your area.

Employers often also have a budget for employee learning and education. If you're interested in a work-related book, a subscription to a learning website, or attending a conference or training program, ask your employer to pay for it.

ESSENTIAL

Organizations managing an international workforce can find it difficult to create fair programs for home office expenses. An employee in Seattle may have better access to certain supplies compared with someone in, say, Honduras. To make it more equitable, some organizations offer a flat monthly benefit for a variety of expenses. It's part of your compensation, so claim it!

Optimizing At-Home Ergonomics

When setting up a remote workstation, most of the work of making sure it's ergonomic falls on you, the worker. If you can get a consultation with an ergonomics specialist, that person will help you make adjustments so that your desk is the right height for your chair, your chair has sufficient back and arm support, your monitor is at a good level for your eyes, and so forth. You might be on your own, though.

Fixing up a home workspace to be ergonomic isn't nearly as complicated as it sounds, but it does take some effort and work.

FACT

Ergonomics is the applied science of designing and arranging things people use, usually in workplace settings, so that the interaction between people and things is efficient and safe. In office work, it's principally seen as a way to prevent repetitive stress syndrome as well as head, neck, and back pain from sitting improperly or for too long.

Picture Yourself in the Driver's Seat

Ergonomics experts sometimes make the analogy that sitting at your desk is like sitting in the driver's seat of a vehicle. When you get into a car, you adjust the seat so you can reach the pedals comfortably and see the road well. You might adjust the headrest, steering wheel, and the height of the seat belt over your shoulder. You look in the rearview and side-view mirrors and adjust them until you have a clear line of sight behind you and to either side of the vehicle.

If you got into a car and adjusted only the seat or only the mirrors, you wouldn't be in a very safe or comfortable position for driving. You need to check and adjust all the movable parts. The same thing goes for setting up a workstation. Just having a good chair doesn't cut it. You have to look at the whole picture and account for all the moving parts.

Neutral and Supported

Two key words in creating an ergonomic workspace are "neutral" and "supported." Every part of your body should be in a neutral position, meaning not stressed or requiring a lot of effort, and supported.

For example, the best office chairs have a headrest so that you can lean back and provide support for your head and take pressure off your neck. Your chair should support your legs, back, and arms. Your feet should rest comfortably on the floor or a footrest with adequate support under them.

FACT

Depending on how often you work remotely, you might not need much fancy furniture or equipment at all. Kitchen and dining room tables are typically built to be at a height where most people can rest their arms and hands flat. That's perfectly fine for typing on a thin laptop.

You need to consider and adjust for your head and neck; back and posture (including hips and spine); arms, wrists, and hands; and legs and feet. Lastly is the issue of circulation and movement, which has less to do with setting up equipment to be ergonomic and more to do with taking regular breaks and changing your body's position.

Head and Neck

If you've ever done yoga, you may have heard about "stacking" your head and neck. That's precisely the way to prevent injury to your neck, shoulders, and back when sitting for long periods of time. Putting the head vertical to the neck, as if balancing the head there, creates the least amount of strain.

What you don't want is to be tilting your head back severely to look up or craning your neck forward. Those head positions typically occur while looking at a monitor that's not at the proper eye level.

Back and Posture

To sit properly and ergonomically for office work, your body should be leaning back slightly, *not* perpendicular to the floor. Leaning back slightly allows your chair and back cushion to do their job of supporting your lower back.

When you lean back a little bit, your hip points should tilt up and back rather than forward. In other words, the base of your spine curves toward the front of your chair rather than the back.

> **ALERT**
>
> In an ergonomic office setup, if you were to draw a straight line parallel to the floor from your eyes to your monitor, your eyes would be about two to three inches below the top of the monitor. That way, you can look straight ahead and easily keep your head and neck in a neutral position.
>
> In addition to getting your line of sight just right, don't forget to look away from your screen from time to time, focus on something that's a different distance than your monitor, and blink regularly.

Arms, Wrists, and Hands

When you're seated, your arms, wrists, and hands should be in a neutral position and well supported. When you're typing and using a mouse, everything from the elbow down should be close to parallel with the table or floor, with the hand, wrist, and forearm practically flush with one another. Avoid hinging at the wrist, which creates strain and circulation problems over time.

> **ESSENTIAL**
>
> A back cushion designed for office work can make an average chair much more comfortable and ergonomic. If you don't have one or are still shopping around, use a small pillow or a rolled-up towel for lumbar support until you find a cushion you like.

Keep your arms in a neutral and fairly straight direction as they come out from your body too. Don't let your elbows jut out to either side. If you find your typing position puts your hands too close together, look into an ergonomic keyboard or a split keyboard. They spread out the keys to make the left and right sides farther apart. Most ergonomic keyboards also have a curve to them that prevents you from hinging your wrists upward.

Legs and Feet

When you're seated, the front edge of your chair should not hit the back of your knees—there should be a gap—because it can reduce blood flow and cause swelling in the ankles and feet. Adjust the chair until you have a good fit, or use an appropriately sized back cushion to scoot yourself forward.

If your feet don't fully reach the floor, you'll need a footrest. Having support under your feet allows your posture to be correct and your back to get the support it needs from the chair too.

Movement and Circulation

No matter how ergonomically correct your workstation is, you still need to get up and move about once every twenty minutes (in an ideal world) to get your blood flowing. These movement sessions do not have to be long, but you do need to stand, stretch, blink, and shift your gaze to give your eyes a rest fairly regularly.

Taking even a one-minute break to stand and roll your neck can help. Even better, every two or three breaks, walk around for a few minutes to get a drink of water, make a cup of coffee or tea, open a window, or do another quick, healthy task. Frequent movement in between long periods of sitting promotes circulation, comfort, and productivity, all while decreasing the risk of injury.

CHAPTER 4

Learning the Art of Remote Communication

For remote teams to be successful, everyone must be highly attuned to what makes communication effective and clear. How do they become highly attuned? They talk about communication a lot. Communicating clearly is a practice. It takes constant learning and attention. For remote teams, it's better to overcommunicate and emphasize the need for clear communication at all times than to correct poor communication after the fact.

Remote Teams Must Overcommunicate

Remote teams intentionally overcommunicate. They talk about overcommunicating. Then they overcommunicate. Then they point out how they overcommunicated. "Look at us!" they cheer. "Overcommunicating!" Virtual high fives all round.

Overcommunicating is indeed something to celebrate in remote teams because the opposite, undercommunicating, can easily leave employees feeling lost, isolated, and confused.

Capturing the Mood

Employees in location-based jobs pick up on signals that indicate when work is going well. People smile in the hallways. You might hear in casual conversations that work is on an upward trajectory. When morale is high, people tend to be in a good mood. The opposite happens when there are major problems in location-based work. People feel the stress and are less likely to strike up a casual conversation. You feel the tension through other people's body language, facial expressions, and how they speak to one another.

In remote work, there's very little ambient atmosphere to signal when business is running smoothly or nearing panic mode. The only way to know is if someone tells you, which is one reason overcommunicating is so important.

Written Communication Has Its Limits

Another reason to overcommunicate is because writing, which is the primary form of communication in remote work, has its limitations. Writing is excellent at capturing information that people can refer back to, although when you have many different places where you store written information, it can be a challenge to find what you need. Therefore, making the same information available in multiple places is one way to overcommunicate.

Written communication is also less effective than in-person communication when it comes to conveying the complexities of human emotion, unless you write at length. Long-form essays aren't exactly the most effective way to communicate in business, however. Who has time to read when they're trying to work? So remote workers turn to other ways to express emotion that are clear but also succinct.

What does it mean to overcommunicate in practice?

Go Ahead and Repeat Yourself

For starters, overcommunicating is about repeating yourself.

When teams keep a lot of information in writing, something's bound to get buried and overlooked. When people repeat themselves by communicating the same information in a variety of ways, it increases the chances that everyone will receive the message or be able to find the information when they need it.

Imagine a scenario in which you are about to take two weeks off work. You've planned a vacation. You've worked hard to make sure that you're caught up on all your work and asked a colleague to fill in any gaps in your coverage while you're out. Your boss approved your time off weeks ago.

The thing about time off is everyone remembers their own, and no one remembers anyone else's. Just because your boss approved your days off and your colleagues agreed to cover for you doesn't mean they'll remember. So you overcommunicate by repeating yourself. You post in your team messaging app a reminder of the days you'll be out and set your away message to indicate the date you'll be back. You mention it again in the next team meeting and at your weekly one-on-one with your manager. On your last working day before your time off starts, you post a message in the team messaging channel: "Reminder: I'll be **out on vacation starting tomorrow, January 10, and back January 25**. I won't be checking messages or email regularly. Tisha will be covering all matters related to Project Y."

For people who are new to remote work, overcommunicating might feel like nagging. It takes time to get used to it. When you overcommunicate, however, you help make sure that information is clear, received, and available to reference if anyone forgets. In a remote environment, overcommunication happens in multiple channels: in a video meeting, via direct messages with your teammates and boss, on your team's shared calendar, in your team's messaging channel, and in your status indicator in collaboration apps. By delivering and recording information in multiple places, you increase the chances that others will see and hear your message rather than being caught unaware or having to search for it.

State the Obvious

Another example of intentional overcommunication is to state the obvious. When things are going well, say so. When collaboration is awkward, address it.

There's a saying that good work goes unnoticed, which may be true, but it's a terrible way to run a business. In location-based work, word usually gets around when someone has a major win. People hear about it, even if it isn't celebrated. It's a smile in the hallway or a watercooler conversation: "Hey, I heard you're managing Project Y. Everyone's really impressed with it!" But in remote work, you might not get any positive feedback at all, unless people intentionally make the effort to overcommunicate and say so.

In location-based work, plenty of mildly uncomfortable situations blow over with time or exposure. The more you see someone and get to know them, the easier it is to accept their unique behaviors, actions, mannerisms, ways of speaking, and so on. However, in remote work, a short and uncomfortable interaction can have lingering effects, unless you overcommunicate by stating the obvious and acknowledging the situation. That way, everyone can talk it out and make sure that their working relationships stay positive, professional, and comfortable.

Assume Good Intent

When people overcommunicate, they talk and write and share *a lot*. In the course of communicating so much, someone is bound to say something that comes off wrong or rubs someone the wrong way.

Before reacting to a comment that doesn't sit right, pause, and assume the other person had good intentions. Things come out wrong. It happens. People get stressed and say things in a clumsy way. Take a moment to decide the right way to address it, perhaps privately. But you can't go into an air-clearing conversation, especially in a remote work environment, if you already assume the person had a bad intention. The only way to build trust is to be open-minded to the idea that the heart of the problem is a miscommunication or a mistake, not a bad intention.

Talk about What to Talk About

As much as everyone in a remote organization may be encouraged to overcommunicate, it is possible to go too far or share information that's not appropriate for everyone. The way to mediate this potential problem is to talk about what to talk about.

Airing every single little grievance doesn't lead to an effective work culture. It's common in remote work to corral nonwork-related discussions, like those about news or pets, into contained message boards so that only people who opt in to those discussions are subjected to them.

ALERT

With some human resources matters, such as reporting a workplace incident or filing a formal complaint, you may not have any control over who gets to know what, depending on laws and organizational policy. Ask your HR contact how information will be shared prior to describing it in detail so that you can make an informed decision about how to proceed.

In addition to knowing what to talk about, remote workers also need to be explicit when information isn't for public consumption. If there's something you want to share with limited individuals, such as a personal matter that affects your work, you need to say so and name the people who know. Make it clear. If someone shares information with you that sounds personal, ask if you're supposed to keep it confidential.

A Look at Synchronous versus Asynchronous Communication

One of the many ways remote teams keep lines of communication clear is to talk openly about synchronous versus asynchronous communication. Most businesses use both, but remote organizations tend to use a lot more asynchronous communication than location-based groups.

Synchronous Communication

Synchronous communication happens in real time or near real time between two or more people. A face-to-face conversation is synchronous. Telephone calls and video calls are synchronous. In those instances, people have body language, tone of voice, and other cues that add to the communication. Synchronous communication can also happen without facial expressions or voices, however. For example, real-time collaborative document editing can be synchronous.

In a synchronous discussion, all parties can respond in real time to ask questions, clarify points, add new information, and so forth. Those are all wonderful advantages. The conversation can be fluid.

Synchronous communication also has disadvantages. For one, because people are expected to react and reply in real time, they don't have the luxury of time to think about what they want to say and how to put it. Synchronous communication can also be more taxing for introverts and people who are less experienced in the language. When synchronous discussions are oral, there's not usually a recording of the conversation, and, even if there is, it's difficult and time-consuming to transcribe it and make it available to others, much less search it for the information you need.

Asynchronous Communication

Asynchronous communication does not happen in real time. Sending a letter by mail is asynchronous, as is email. Leaving someone a voicemail is asynchronous. Forums and message boards are asynchronous (not to be confused with team messaging apps, which can be used both synchronously and asynchronously).

As you might have guessed, most of the advantages and disadvantages of asynchronous communication are the opposite of those for synchronous communication.

In asynchronous conversations, everyone can take their time to think about what they want to say and phrase it accordingly. Asynchronous communication always produces a record, which people can review and reference for details. Having a record also makes asynchronous conversations more accessible to anyone who needs to take their time with understanding the message.

A disadvantage of asynchronous communication is that there is no immediate feedback. Usually, you have to wait for an unknown amount of time to get a reply, which can cause delays. If someone asks for clarification or raises a new point in a reply, there could be even more delays in the conversation.

Because asynchronous communication causes delays, some remote organizations have a "default to action" policy. The details of the policy will vary by organization, but the gist of it is this: If work is blocked because you're waiting for an answer or an approval, and you can guess with some amount of certainty how to proceed (and there's usually a number, like 90 percent), go ahead and take action.

If Either, Assume Asynchronous

Some methods of communication can be either asynchronous or synchronous, depending on how people use them. For example, if you send a text message or instant message to someone and they reply immediately, you're now in a synchronous chat. If you intend to continue the chat synchronously, you need to tell the other person (i.e., overcommunicate your intention). That way, if the other party has to step away from the conversation, they'll tell you first instead of unintentionally leaving you hanging.

When you don't know whether the other person will be immediately available, err on the side of caution and assume the conversation will be asynchronous until proven otherwise.

What Does Transparency Mean in a Remote Work Environment?

A tenet of remote work culture is transparency. Founders of the most influential remote-first organizations built them to be intentionally transparent. In this context, "transparent" means that the organization values open communication and prioritizes making information accessible. Transparency takes many forms in remote work, but it chiefly comes in two flavors: internal and external.

Internal transparency involves open communication and information-sharing within the organization. Internal transparency is usually what people are referring to when they talk about transparency in remote work.

External transparency involves how much information the organization makes public about its culture, values, practices, earnings, employee benefits, salaries, leadership decisions, and so forth.

> **ESSENTIAL**
>
> While transparency is largely viewed as a positive trait for organizations, there is a downside. It generates an overwhelming amount of information. If you feel like you're drowning in information at a remote job, take a deep breath and know that it's normal.

Internal Transparency

Internal transparency, or transparency within an organization, goes a long way to building trust and confidence among the leadership team, management, and employees. To reiterate, internal transparency emphasizes the availability and access to information. While some information may come in the form of a presentation from the founders or executive team, more often information is stored somewhere that's accessible to employees, putting the onus on them to seek it out.

A lot of top-down transparency is financial, such as specific numbers related to how well the organization is doing or how current financial figures compare to previous projections. Is the organization meeting its goals? Is it profitable? This type of transparency builds trust and confidence because you, the employee, have hard data related to how secure you can feel in the stability of the organization and thus your job.

In conjunction with financial look-back data, a transparent organization will openly share whether it has met its past goals, as well as its future goals, plans, and aspirations. That information gives you a clear sense of the mission and path for growth, as well as a better understanding of how your specific job duties contribute to the organization's success.

Everything described so far generally comes from the highest leadership in an organization, such as the executive team or founders. A common way for them to share this information is through an all-hands meeting, also known as a town hall or company-wide meeting. In other words, it's a meeting where everyone in the organization is not only invited but expected to attend. How often all-hands meetings take place depends on the size of the organization and how much the leadership team has to share. Anywhere from once a week to twice a year would be considered normal. Big, important meetings like these are often recorded so that anyone who cannot attend always has the option of watching the meeting on their own time. That's another example of transparency—making information easily accessible to all.

Another form of internal transparency is giving employees clear performance expectations. For many years, there was a tendency in startup culture to tell employees to write their own job descriptions. On the one hand, deciding what you want to do and how gives you autonomy. On the other hand, it doesn't set you up for success, because your assumptions and expectations might be wildly different from what the leadership team wants you to do. You're in a much better position when you know what's expected, and it's even better if it's objective and measurable. Having regular meetings with your supervisor or manager is part of this—more on meetings in remote work culture later.

ALERT

When it comes to identifying and tracking goals transparently, a popular method many organizations use is OKRs, which stands for "objectives and key results" (popularized at Google). In this method, teams identify, write down, and measure progress toward goals. Experts caution that in most cases, OKRs are not helpful for individuals; they're really meant for teams and departments. So beware of having to write OKRs for your own work.

Organizations make good on their promise to be transparent in other ways too. Sometimes it's as simple as making an organization's values, priorities, and plans available for employees to see and reference. Similarly, employee handbooks, guides, and policies should be easily accessible to all employees at any time. Remote organizations, which are used to sharing documents electronically, tend to be pretty good at it.

External Transparency

In general, external transparency isn't as central to remote work as internal transparency, but a few companies setting trends in remote work culture take it pretty seriously.

External transparency means sharing information with the public—which includes clients, competitors, and members of the media—that isn't normally expected of an organization. Examples of information that might be shared externally include limited financial data (successes at the least), company values, future plans and visions, and employee benefits. Sure sounds like promotional material to wow customers, attract top talent, and build a brand image, doesn't it?

Some amount of public gloating can be good for everyone. Take for example remote organizations that publicize employee benefits. If you could work for any remote company, wouldn't you want to work for one that has a generous time-off policy, a paid sabbatical every few years, a supportive parental leave plan, and other benefits? If other remote-first organizations start to match these benefits to attract top talent, too, that benefits employees everywhere.

External transparency can backfire. When leadership teams share their decision-making thought process with the public and it is not well received, everyone in the organization can feel like the spotlight of shame is on them. Do you defend your organization, add your voice to the dissenters, or try to lie low? How will your employer or the public judge you for your response? It can put you in a compromising situation.

Tips for Being Clear Yet Concise in Written Communication

Knowing that you should be clear and concise in your written communication is much different from learning how to do it. It takes effort to learn and practice to get better.

"Good writing" is contextual. A well-written academic research paper has a completely different structure, tone, and purpose than a news article. Remote work has a unique context for its written communication. Who will read what I write? When and where will they read it? What information does the person need to understand, and how can I deliver it to them clearly?

You can become a wonderfully effective communicator in a remote job by learning how to:

- Write in plain language.
- Assume a global audience.
- Use formatting to make information clear.
- Revise your writing before sharing it.
- Not fear the edit button.

Use Plain Language

The Plain Writing Act of 2010 is based on principles of the plain language movement, which has grown and is sometimes now known as plain language studies. It's extremely useful and relevant in remote work communication.

Plain language is written communication that:

- Contains specific information that's relevant to the reader
- Is logically arranged and easy to follow
- Shows clear thinking
- Uses principles of plain language, which include using short sentences and simple words

When writing in plain language, say what you mean, avoid synonyms, and stick to facts. Plain language writing allows the reader to understand a message clearly after reading it just once.

Nobody's born knowing how to write in plain language. It's a skill that you learn and develop. In remote work, it's worth finding a course or a few articles that teach plain language writing so you can practice it and improve.

Write for a Global Audience

Remote workforces, as mentioned, are often global. When organizations can hire the best talent from anywhere in the world, they do. In this increasingly globalized workforce, remote workers need to learn to write for a global audience.

Writing in plain language and writing for a global audience go hand in hand. Clear writing for a global audience assumes that the reader could be located anywhere, may have a different first language than you, and may have different cultural experiences, contexts, and values.

What are the hallmarks of clear and effective communication in a globalized setting?

- **Time zone awareness** is one. Always give dates and times in a clear format that anyone anywhere in the world can understand. Avoid time and date words that are relative, like "tomorrow." Similarly, avoid phrases that are regional, like "Friday week" (the British English way of saying "one week from this coming Friday").
- **Dates** are another area where it's important to be precise. Anyone will be able to recognize that "4 May" and "May 4" are the same date. But 4/5 and 5/4 are not mutually intelligible.
- **Seasonal references** are confusing and unclear in a globalized environment too. Seasons aren't the same across borders and lines of latitude. Someone in Malaysia might not know if "summer" means the hottest months for the northern or southern hemisphere, much less which months those are.
- **Idioms, metaphors (especially sports metaphors), and flowery language** are best saved for awards speeches and other special events, like baby showers and retirement celebrations, when putting in extra effort to be eloquent might be appreciated.

Formatting: Paragraph Returns, Boldface, Bullet Points

Formatting goes a long way to making business communication clear, concise, and effective. Perhaps the three most common types of formatting that make a message clear are paragraph returns, boldface, and bullet points.

Paragraph returns transform long blocks of text into shorter groups of sentences that are easier to read and understand. Boldface, or bold, styling puts emphasis on words to make them jump out. Bullet points let you highlight key ideas in an easy-to-read list.

Other helpful formatting features for business communication include code snippet (a style used on short lines of code to make them distinct from your message), code block (similar to a code snippet, but for multiple lines of code), and block quote (which offsets some language that you are quoting to make it distinct from your message).

Write, Reread, Revise

Before sending a message or contributing to a shared document, take a few moments to reread and revise your text to make sure it is clear and concise. Applying formatting, such as boldface and making bullet lists, is an extremely effective way to reread your message and check whether you should revise it. If you can easily apply boldface to the most important parts, it's probably clear and concise. If you have to jump around to put important words in bold, you probably should revise.

Here's an example of the same message written and formatted to be unclear (first) and clear (second):

- We're thinking of having a meeting on **Friday** in the afternoon, probably **3:00 p.m.** local time for the folks in the UK, since we're going to talk about **their project**. Jean is sending the details.

■ The **London team project meeting** will be **Friday, May 14, at 3:00 p.m. (15:00) GMT** via video call. The agenda, link for the call, and other details will come in an **email invitation from Jean**.

In the first example, the message doesn't say which Friday the meeting will be held. The time and time zone information are not written clearly. The message doesn't specify where the meeting will take place, what it will address, or how Jean will send the details.

In the second message, important information is grouped together, making it easy to put it in boldface, and that makes it stand out. The necessary information is clear and succinct. The message could have been longer and even more detailed. For example, it could have included some of the agenda items. But because it's short, anyone can read it once, get the necessary information quickly, and get back to doing their job.

Sending a clear message the first time saves time in the long run for everyone. Reading and revising your written communication doesn't take a lot of time to do, and you'll improve at it and get faster the more you do it.

Use the Edit Button in Team Messaging Apps

Everyone makes mistakes. Everyone hits Send prematurely. It happens. If you catch a mistake before hitting Send, revise your message rather than sending a second message with a correction or clarification. It is much clearer and more efficient to have the first message be correct than to send two messages that people must read and synthesize to get the right information.

Team messaging apps, such as Slack and Microsoft Teams, let you revise a message after you've posted it. If you edit that message, the system shows a little note next to the post that indicates it's been edited.

Editing a message in a team messaging app works only if you catch the error quickly or if you're sure other people have not seen the message yet. For example, if you post a message to a public channel and realize an hour later that you ought to correct or clarify a point, people may have already seen the first message, and they may not pay attention to an edit. In that case, it's better to provide a separate correction. If you send a direct message to someone who is currently off-line (according to the indicators in the app), you can be fairly certain that they haven't seen the message yet, meaning you can revise your message or delete it and write a new one.

Embracing Emoji, Reacji, and Exclamation Points!

Do you love emoji, reacji, and exclamation points? No? Well, in remote work, you might have to learn to love them!

FACT

Reacji are emoji reactions. In other words, when one person posts a message on a communication channel, other people can respond to it with a heart, smiley face, or other emoji. Reacji indicate emotion, reaction, support, or sometimes an answer, as in a checkmark in response to a request to do a task.

So much communication in remote work is written. Remote organizations use team messaging apps, shared files, handbooks and documentation, email, and other written communication because it supports asynchronous work. When coworkers don't see one another face-to-face regularly or get to know each other on a deeply personal level (which happens in location-based work too), it becomes very hard if not impossible to interpret tone in written communication.

To be kind, show enthusiasm, and indicate tone, use emoji, reacji, and exclamation points with abundance. It may feel out of character, but the purpose is to make your communication as clear as possible to others. It's not about you; it's about everyone else, and these tools do a lot of heavy lifting in written communication.

Never Dangle Feedback

The protocol for offering and receiving feedback in location-based work is completely different from how it should be done in remote work.

In location-based work, where two people can have a face-to-face conversation without much planning, the protocol is to always ask first whether the recipient has time to talk about the relevant matter. Then both parties can decide on a mutually agreed-upon time and place to have a discussion. It might be "here and now" for brief conversations, but sometimes "later and off-site" works better.

In remote work, where people might be working asynchronously, always indicate that there is feedback and then give the feedback *at the same time*. Never dangle feedback by sending a message that you have feedback without saying what it is. You risk leaving someone wondering whether there's bad news and how long it'll be until they receive it. That's a terrible state for anyone.

If you have feedback to give, either wait until you are having a synchronous conversation with the other person or take the time to write out your feedback carefully in a way that allows the other person to read it and absorb it without being left with questions. Good feedback should be clear, relevant, and not personal.

Feedback can be constructive, meaning one person is pointing out an action or behavior that's potentially problematic. Feedback can also be positive praise. When you have positive feedback, front-load the praise so that the reader knows immediately that the news is good.

Here is a very simple format for giving feedback: When X happens, the result is Y. From there, you can add to the beginning or end as necessary to clarify the situation or better describe the preferred outcome.

Here's an example of positive feedback: Hi, Boss! Thank you for pointing out my recent successes in the latest team meeting. When you acknowledge those successes to the whole team, I feel confident in my work and know that my contributions matter. I really appreciate it!

Here's an example of constructive feedback: Hi, Boss. I have some feedback about a comment from the last team meeting. When you acknowledged to the whole team that I missed a deadline without explaining all the details, it caught me off guard and made me feel like I had let down the team. I understand why you brought it up, but in the future, would you mind addressing these issues with me in a one-on-one first? That way, I know it's coming and I can add the appropriate context so that my colleagues will continue to trust my work.

Not all feedback is suitable for asynchronous delivery. Sometimes a synchronous conversation is much better. In a synchronous conversation, both parties have an opportunity to ask and answer questions. For example, if two people experienced the same event differently, summarizing it in an asynchronous message isn't going to help.

However you choose to give feedback, be careful not to dangle it before providing it.

CHAPTER 5

Etiquette for Video and Audio Calls

Saying there's an etiquette for a video or audio call is like saying there are rules for how to write a resume. There aren't. There are only guidelines, and those guidelines change depending on your industry, purpose, and other factors. Plus, the same way you should write a custom resume for every job application, the specific etiquette for a video or audio call changes for each one. There are some common practices and trends for various types of calls in the remote landscape, however, and knowing about them can help you navigate your calls.

Camera On or Off? How to Decide When to Use Video

For video calls, should you turn your camera on or leave it off? It depends on how many people are on the call, who arranges it, and whether it's a regular recurring call or a one-off. And if you have personal reasons for wanting to leave your camera off, you should almost always be able to do so.

ALERT

Ultimately, whether you feel comfortable turning on your video camera is up to you. The particulars of your personal life, physical abilities and disabilities, and surroundings may influence your decision too.

When a lot of people are on a call, say, more than about a dozen, you can usually opt out of being on camera with no consequences. The same goes for presentation-style calls, such as town halls, lectures, most large group trainings, and seminars. As long as you aren't expected to participate, you can safely assume that in any large group call, turning on your camera is entirely optional.

In small-group calls or one-on-one calls, whether you turn on your camera may depend on who arranged the call or is hosting it. Typically, the host sets the tone. If someone invites you to a call and they have their camera off, turn yours off as well. If you've scheduled the call and are meant to steer the conversation, the other parties will watch whether you have your camera on, and, if they're experienced in remote work, they'll do whatever you do. An even better solution: Overcommunicate by stating plainly in the meeting or call invitation whether you intend to have your camera on or off. "Let's keep our cameras off for this one," or "I'm planning to have my camera on for this call, but feel free to leave yours off if you prefer." Making it clear to everyone in advance helps a lot.

For small-group calls with familiar faces, such as your immediate teammates and other colleagues you know reasonably well, you probably have the option to have your camera on or off. In these sorts of settings, people will be happy to give you a pass if you prefer to leave your camera off from time to time. That said, if everyone else defaults to having their cameras on, then you should consider turning yours on at least some of the time as well.

If you have a concrete reason to leave your camera off, however, by all means do so. It will probably help with group cohesion if you acknowledge it to your colleagues, even if you give a nonspecific reason. For example, you could say something like "Just to let you all know, I'm leaving my camera off because I have some ongoing personal/medical/family issues." Whether you share more is up to you, but simply addressing it goes a long way to making it a nonissue rather than letting people guess what's up.

QUESTION

What if I can't tell from a meeting invitation whether I'll need to have my camera on?

If you aren't sure, assume it's cameras on. That way you'll be prepared rather than caught off guard. And if everyone else has their cameras off then you can leave yours off, too, and it's a bonus.

Addressing Privacy Concerns for Video Calls

By joining a video call and turning your camera on, you're giving up some amount of privacy. For example, if you work from home, turning a camera on in your personal space can be extremely revealing and make you feel vulnerable. You could be sharing information about yourself and your private life that you'd rather keep private, such as the appearance of your home and who's in it.

These concerns are valid. In an ideal world, you would always have the option to bow out of using your video camera for a call. But this isn't an ideal world, and there can be consequences to not ever turning on your video.

If you work from your home full-time, it's highly advisable that you find a comfortable place or a method for taking video calls with the camera on. Someone who never joins a call by video stands out, and not in a good way. You really have to have exceptional circumstances for getting away with never being on video.

People who work from home only part-time might find their colleagues are more forgiving of their camera-off moments, in part because they put in face time with these colleagues when they're at the office or shared work location.

No matter how often you work remotely, it's better to figure out a way to incorporate video comfortably, at least some of the time, than to never show your face on camera.

Take Video Calls Outside the Home

One simple solution is to leave home when you have a scheduled video call and take it from somewhere else. For this solution to work, you need to know about the call in advance and have a place to go that's fairly quiet and you can talk out loud. The place must also have reliable Internet service.

You can book time in a conference room at a coworking space for this purpose. Or maybe there's a good café nearby that isn't too noisy or has outdoor space where you can speak at a conversational volume without disturbing others.

Use a Virtual or Blurred Background

Many video calling apps now include an option to apply a virtual background or blur your background. A virtual background is an image, whether still or animated, that digitally appears behind you. The app intelligently detects your face and body to keep them on camera but replaces everything else with the background image. When you apply a virtual background, no one can see your actual surroundings, giving you greater privacy.

Another option in many apps is to blur your background. If a virtual background sounds too gimmicky, the blurred background is a better option. It works in nearly the same way, with the software intelligently detecting your face and body to preserve them in the video, but it makes everything else around you look really fuzzy.

Set Up a Standing Room Divider

You can also physically block people on a call from seeing your surroundings by setting up a standing room divider, such as a Japanese folding screen.

Having a divider also signals to other people who might share your space, like roommates and partners, that you're on a call and they shouldn't interrupt you.

Preparing for a Video Call

Before any business call, you need to prepare. Preparation includes checking your software, software settings, surroundings, personal appearance, and lastly your audio and video equipment. Beyond that, you need to prepare for the content of the call (i.e., the purpose of the meeting—but more on that part later).

The longer you work remotely, the easier and quicker it will be to set up for calls, at least for recurring calls. Recurring calls are the ones that repeat on your calendar, such as team meetings and one-on-ones with your manager. It gets easier to prepare for those calls because you'll use the same software and equipment every time and you'll establish a pattern. You might also be more comfortable with these familiar faces and therefore spend less time tidying up your surroundings and yourself prior to the call. Calls with external business partners might require more formality in your personal presentation.

ESSENTIAL

Video calling software is sometimes also referred to as video calling apps or webinar software/apps. You have probably heard of or used many of these brands, like Zoom, Google Meet, Microsoft Teams (which doubles as a team messaging app), RingCentral, BlueJeans, GoToMeeting, and Webex, among many others.

Software and Settings

Before any call, check that the software (meaning the app you'll use to connect to the call) is installed and updated. Give yourself at least five minutes to check for and run updates, though ten is better. It's not the end of the world if you don't run an update right away, but it's good to get in the habit of checking and running updates regularly because they might contain a security fix or a new feature that you will need to participate in the call.

You also need to check the app's settings, which is more important if you're hosting or cohosting the call rather than joining as a participant. If you're hosting or cohosting, verify that the security and privacy settings are what you want them to be. For example, will the participants' cameras and microphones be turned off automatically when they join? Do participants have to register or provide their name before connecting? Do you need to record the call so that anyone who can't join has a video of it to watch later?

ESSENTIAL

The best thing you can do before taking or making video calls is familiarize yourself with the video calling software. Every app is different, though most of them let you choose who can join the call, and have auto-settings to adjust for loud noises, low lighting, and the like. You need to know about these features to use them correctly.

Whatever app your team uses most, set aside some time to learn about its core features and settings. It's really worth your while to learn what you can.

Even though your team will likely have a preferred meeting app, you might still have to use other apps with outside parties, such as clients and other collaborators. Anytime you have a call with a new app, take a few minutes beforehand to run through your checklist and make sure you know the basics.

ALERT

Never check that a video calling app works by testing a link someone has sent you well before the scheduled time. Several video calling apps support reusing links, which means you can use the same link for all your meetings. If you "test" a link while another call is in progress, you could end up crashing someone else's meeting.

Surroundings

The next way to prepare for a video call is by checking your surroundings. Do you need to make sure children or pets are content and won't get into trouble? Is the area behind you, which might be on camera, relatively tidy, or do you want to enable a virtual background or blur filter? Will you be more comfortable if you open or close doors and windows?

You don't need to impress anyone when you prepare your surroundings. Rather, the goal is to make sure that nothing from your space, whether visual or aural, is going to distract other people or detract from your contributions.

Personal Appearance

Remote teams tend to be more relaxed in personal appearance than those who work in in-person business settings. There's no need for a dress code when everyone works remotely. How you prepare your physical self to appear on a call is up to you.

Some people enjoy having a reason to dress up or do a little extra grooming, especially when they do it so rarely. If it makes you feel more comfortable or confident, or simply because you like it, go ahead and do those things.

While no one is going to mandate that you dress up for every call, there's certainly a risk to letting your physical appearance go. Looking completely unkempt can draw negative attention or leave people worrying that you're not taking care of yourself. So make yourself presentable. If you can't pull it together once in a while, ask yourself whether you need to take a sick day or leave your camera off.

Audio and Visual Check

The last check before joining any call is to verify that your device and the calling app are set to use the right equipment and that they work. Most apps let you test and preview your audio and video. If you don't see an obvious option to test or run a check, you can probably create a call with no one else on it and get a preview that way.

During this check, you should be able to preview any virtual backgrounds, camera filters, or other special features in the software that you might want to use. Be aware that in some apps, if you apply a filter or virtual background, it automatically reappears on your next call. That's yet another reason to run a quick test.

Tips for Lighting and Camera Angle

Two keys to looking good on a video call are to have adequate lighting on your face and for your head and shoulders to be centered in the frame.

Looking good on a video call isn't about being vain; it's about *not* drawing unnecessary attention to yourself. When you don't take the time to adjust your camera and lighting, other people on the call notice. A camera shot up the nose is noticeable and distracts from the purpose of the call.

FACT

A 2020 Pew Research Center poll found that 65 percent of remote workers viewed video conferencing and instant messaging apps as a good substitute for in-person contact. The survey also showed that women (70 percent) were more likely than men (60 percent) to feel this way about video calling and messaging apps.

Lighting

Setting up lighting for a video call is pretty easy. You want the light to come toward your face rather than be at your back. If there's a window in the space where you take calls, make sure it's facing you or is at your side but not at your back. Natural daylight looks phenomenal on camera, so if you have a window, use it to your advantage.

That said, having bright daylight shine right on your face while you're trying to look at a computer screen can hurt your eyes and dry them out if you do it for long periods. For that reason, you probably don't want to sit facing a window at all times. Instead, set up your workstation so that the window is at your side. If the light is insufficient for video calls in that position, you can always pivot when you have a call. All you have to do is move your chair and turn your computer or laptop ninety degrees. Now that gorgeous light is bathing your face, and you can flip back to your normal position when the call ends.

Turning on overhead lights helps raise the total light level in the room, which you might need, but it doesn't do much to light your face specifically.

Lamps work similarly to daylight, more or less, though the light they provide isn't nearly as lovely as what you get from the sun. If you have a lamp, position it behind your camera so the light shines on your face but not directly on the camera. Table lamps with shades are tricky to use for this purpose, as are desk lamps that point down toward the tabletop. Play with the lighting you have, and always opt for natural sunlight when available over lamps.

> **ESSENTIAL**
>
> If you spend any amount of time doing professional presentations via video call, you need a reliable and consistent light source. Daylight is inconsistent, and lamps aren't designed to light your face to be on camera. The solution? Get a simple ring light. They're relatively inexpensive and compact, and they provide soft directional lighting on your face.

With today's webcams and video calling software, you don't have to put in a lot of effort to make your setup adequate. Most video calling apps have an option in the settings to automatically adjust for low light. Enabling that button does a lot of work for you. If you have it enabled and you still look dark in the preview window on your screen, switch the low light adjustment setting to manual and dial it up a bit. You can also turn up the brightness of your own screen because when it's dark, you might still look shaded in the video camera preview window even if you have reasonable ambient lighting.

Camera Angle

A good camera angle shows your face head-on and usually includes a fair amount of your neck and shoulders too. It will change depending on how close or wide the shot is. If the camera isn't too tight on your face, try to position yourself so that either your nose or chin is more or less in the center.

The camera should be head-on, meaning not angled low and pointing up at you, which is what happens when you have a laptop on your lap. The camera shouldn't be too high above you either. Why does it matter? When the camera is at the right level, you look more natural and relaxed than if it's at an unusual level. Plus, as mentioned, it isn't a distraction, whereas a bad camera angle is.

If you set up a home office with your computer or laptop in a good position for ergonomics, the top of your screen should be nearly at eye level already, which is what you want because built-in cameras are usually right at the top. If you have an external camera, it's probably attached to the top of your monitor or display, which is exactly where you want it.

If you're working on a laptop that's sitting on a table and you don't have a laptop riser, stack a few books or grab a small box and put your laptop on top. That's a simple, inexpensive solution for adjusting the height that works just fine for video calls. Be careful that the books or box are wide enough to provide adequate support and won't tip over easily!

When and When Not to Mute

There's a pretty simple rule to figuring out when to mute your microphone and when not to mute: Do what everyone else is doing. In all seriousness, if you're new to a team, pay attention to when and why other people mute their mics and follow suit.

Commonly, people who are experienced with video calls will mute their microphones if:

- The call is with a large group ("large" being a relative term)
- An individual has background noise that's difficult to silence, such as kids, pets, or the buzz of a lawn mower or air traffic outside

There is a reason for people on a call to leave their microphones unmuted, however. It allows for a more free-flowing conversation, with interjections and questions. If you have to think about unmuting yourself before jumping in to ask for a clarification, you might be less likely to do it. Having to mute and unmute adds a layer of inconvenience and a slight delay that could lead you to change your mind about asking an otherwise good question. It's hard to foster real discussion when each person has to click a button before speaking and double-check that it's their turn to speak.

Sometimes teams have unspoken rules about when they mute or leave themselves unmuted. A team with a strong remote culture will make the rules explicit. But if you have any doubts, just ask if everyone prefers to mute microphones when they're not talking or to leave them on. You could also ask if they have any guidance on how many people need to be in a call before everyone mutes.

> **ESSENTIAL**
>
> If everyone on a call leaves their microphone open except you, briefly tell everyone why you're muting. Use the chat function if you don't want to interrupt, or pipe up when you have a chance. A team with a strong remote culture shouldn't need an explanation—they should trust that you are exercising good judgment—but it never hurts to overcommunicate.

Tips for Better Audio Quality

Like everything else in remote-work life, getting good audio quality in meetings can be an ongoing process. It takes a little trial and error to acquire and adjust your equipment, learn which settings work best, find a good place to take calls, and so forth.

To get the best audio quality on calls:

- Use headphones and a microphone
- Be careful of your microphone input
- Enable noise-reduction settings
- Minimize echoes and ambient noises in your physical setting

Use Headphones and a Microphone

Full-time remote employees should consider adding an audio headset to their home office or remote office equipment. Headphones make call audio much clearer, although there are plenty of reasons you might choose not to use them, such as accessibility issues or comfort.

The microphone on a headset cuts down significantly on environmental noises, allowing your colleagues to hear you clearly. The earphones prevent feedback because the audio of the call isn't being played audibly in the room and therefore can't be picked up accidentally by the mic. Earphones also might make it easier for you to hear your colleagues clearly, in part because you can more finely adjust the volume settings.

Look for a pair of headphones that includes a microphone, unless you have a separate need for a stand-alone high-quality mic, such as hosting a podcast or doing regular media interviews. For most people, the microphone that's included in a headset is more than sufficient.

A decent pair of headphones with a microphone doesn't have to be expensive. A standard wired headphone set with a little microphone built into the cord works just as well for business calls as an expensive noise-canceling Bluetooth headphone set. Just make sure the part of the wire that holds the mic doesn't rub against your clothing or hair, or rumble against a zipper, as that makes an incredibly distinctive and distracting noise for everyone else on the call.

You can also buy Bluetooth headphones with a microphone that come with the option to be wired or wireless. Keep in mind that Bluetooth headphones run on battery power and need to be charged regularly, whereas other wired headphone sets are plug-and-play ready.

With Built-In Microphones, Don't Block the Input

If you have to use the built-in microphone on your laptop, computer, or mobile device, make sure nothing is covering it. It's more commonly a problem with laptop and mobile devices than desktop computers.

On a laptop or desktop computer, the microphones (typically there are more than one) aren't usually visible. On older hardware, you might be able to identify where they are by tiny openings somewhere on your device. More often, however, they're tucked somewhere under the laptop casing, such as under or to the side of the keyboard, alongside the speakers, or at the side edge of the device. On mobile devices, such as smartphones and tablets, the microphone is usually housed behind a slitted vent or series of small openings, making it easier to identify the location.

In any event, be mindful of where you rest your forearms or hands, or how you grip your device, as you could block the microphones. Be careful not to place it on a soft surface, like a pillow, couch cushion, or blanket, because that may also inadvertently muffle the microphone.

Enable Noise-Reducing Settings

In the same way that you can enable a setting that automatically corrects for low lighting on a video call, you can often enable a setting to automatically hush ambient noises. Look for noise-reduction settings in two places: the app you use for video calls and your device's sound settings.

In your video calling app, go to the setting called Audio, Sound, or something similar. Look for an option to adjust/reduce/suppress background noise. Some apps let you choose how aggressively to block out extra noises, so pick the level that seems right to you.

The device-level settings for noise reduction are in different places usually for desktop and laptop computers versus mobile devices. On most computers, you'll find a Sound or Audio area in your settings that will likely have some kind of ambient noise-reduction option. On mobile devices, you'll have to look around because the options vary by device. For example, in current iPhones, there's an option in the Accessibility settings under Audio/Visual to reduce ambient noises, but it applies to phone calls only when you lift the device to your ear. With Android phones and tablets, the options vary depending on which specific device you have.

Regardless of whether you have a lot of background noise that you need to tone down, it's a really good idea to be familiar with all these audio settings, as they come in handy for troubleshooting other problems too. For example, they help you choose your headphone set and microphone as the audio output and input, rather than defaulting to the built-in speakers and mic on your device.

Other Ways to Reduce Ambient Noise

Device and app-level settings help reduce ambient noise a great deal, but there are other simple tricks you can use in your own surroundings to make the audio better too.

For starters, close doors and windows for the duration of a call. Turn off fans or other equipment that uses a motor, or move farther away from anything that persistently hums or buzzes, like a refrigerator.

Reduce echo by choosing to take calls in a room that has rugs, blankets, pillows, and furniture. You may have heard stories of people who work in professional spoken audio (audiobook narrators, podcasters, radio reporters) going into their closets to record. Certainly, surrounding yourself with coats and dresses in a tiny space will minimize echoes and ambient noises, though it's overkill for a business call—and it really doesn't go over well for video calls.

How to Incorporate Screen Sharing and Virtual Whiteboarding

Video calling apps offer plenty of features, from breakout rooms to polling. Two features that are worth particular attention in remote work are screen sharing and whiteboarding. Screen sharing is usually built into the video calling app. Virtual whiteboards can be included with some apps, but there are also separate whiteboard apps that integrate with video calling software.

Screen Sharing

Screen sharing allows one participant on a video call to share their computer screen (or a select window) so that everyone else on the call can see it. It's commonly used for presentations (even informal ones without slide decks). You can share your screen and show examples of websites you like for website design inspiration or even play a video for your colleagues while pausing to discuss aspects of it.

Screen sharing is also extremely valuable when it comes to tech troubleshooting. IT teams in remote work environments often have special software that allows them to take control of a person's computer from afar to fix a tricky problem. For more minor concerns, such as asking a colleague how to perform a certain function in an app that your team uses, you don't need an IT expert. But you might need to show another more experienced person what you're looking at while you ask for their help.

Some video calling apps have a lightweight version of the IT remote control tool included. Say a junior designer is sharing their work with a more senior designer by sharing her screen. The senior designer sees a few small tweaks to make but is having a hard time explaining to the junior designer exactly how to do it. The senior designer can, if the video calling app supports it, request remote control of the junior designer's screen and make the changes directly. Once done, the senior designer relinquishes control, and the junior designer is back in command.

Virtual Whiteboarding

Location-based workplaces often have big whiteboards—sometimes physical and sometimes digital—in meeting rooms. During a meeting, people brainstorm or jot down ideas and information. At the end of the meeting, you might snap a picture of the final product or save a copy for virtual boards. Whiteboards are a nice tool to have, but they're even better when incorporated into remote work.

As mentioned, a few video calling apps have a whiteboard option included or offer it as a tandem product (in the case of Google Meet and Jamboard, for instance). Some teams prefer to use stand-alone whiteboarding apps, sometimes also called visual collaboration apps, because they tend to have more features that make it easy to draw, add shapes and arrows, place text, and upload files to a board. The best whiteboarding apps offer seamless integration with the top video calling apps; or they offer a video or audio calling feature of their own. A few examples of whiteboarding apps are Microsoft Whiteboard, Miro, MURAL, and Stormboard.

In remote work, whiteboards must be digital rather than physical. They also don't live in a conference room on an oversized touch screen. They're in an app. These apps usually support collaboration, which means you can share a board with others, and everyone can access the board at any time. Therefore, you have the power to make video meetings more efficient by letting participants contribute to or view the board not only during the call (synchronously) but also before and after (asynchronously).

For example, let's say you're setting up a call to brainstorm ideas for a campaign. In writing up the meeting invitation, you add an agenda and a link to a shared whiteboard. In the agenda, you encourage all the invitees to add some of their ideas to the whiteboard in advance of the actual meeting. By the time of the actual meeting, everyone can jump right into a discussion of the ideas rather than spend time individually thinking up ideas.

Whiteboards also enable overcommunication because they are a place to store information and make it readily available. Any team member who can't join a video call can always review the whiteboard at their convenience.

When to Use Broadcast-Style Conference Calls

In most remote work, broadcast-style conference calls happen much less frequently than other kinds of video and audio calls. If you work in event management, training, or have a supporting role to an executive, however, you will almost certainly need to know when to use them. From time to time, they are applicable in other settings, too, so it's helpful to know what they are and how they're different from regular video calls.

Broadcast calls are what they sound like. One or a select few people host a call as presenters, and everyone else is a listener or viewer. Sometimes at the end participants have an opportunity to ask questions, but even then, the hosts can decide whether to let participants speak in real time or have them submit questions in writing only. In other words, there are strict limits on how listeners and viewers can interact with the presenters.

Broadcast calls are often formal presentations, such as earnings calls or large lecture-style training programs. In a very large organization, town halls might be done in broadcast format.

Because broadcast calls are typically formal, sometimes rehearsed, and otherwise highly produced, they record well. That means you can record the call as a video and share it with anyone who couldn't or didn't want to attend in real time.

For employees, there's yet another benefit of having recordings of these types of calls: If they're boring, you can watch them at an increased playback speed.

CHAPTER 6

Understanding Virtual Collaboration and Working on Teams

In organizations that support remote work, whether people work remotely full-time or in a hybrid setup, all collaboration must be rooted in a remote-first mentality. For collaboration to be successful, it has to support remote workers' participation completely and fully. You should avoid a situation in which an in-office team collaborates in whatever way is easiest for them, while inadvertently forcing anyone who works remotely to put in additional effort or take extra steps to participate and access information. For remote work to work, all collaboration must happen with a remote-first mindset.

What Is Remote Collaboration?

Collaboration is the *how* of work. It's *how* things get done in an organization. And in comparing location-based work to remote work, *how* people work is fundamentally different.

First, what exactly does it mean to collaborate? Collaboration comprises all the ways that people work together. It includes having both informal discussions and formal meetings, providing feedback and direction, sharing files, coauthoring and co-editing, and handing off a project, not to mention using an array of collaboration software that keeps track of who's doing what, the status of their progress, and when they've finished.

Second, why is collaboration important? People don't perform discrete tasks all alone and call it a day. Work gets passed from one person to the next. People come together to discuss ideas, make decisions, and create new things. Junior employees learn from more senior ones how to improve their skills. Even when multiple people complete work separately from one another—for example, one person writes a magazine article and another person draws an illustration for it—their work may still have to come together later in a cohesive way. Very little work happens in complete isolation.

So what is remote collaboration? It's doing all these collaborative activities when people are apart.

ESSENTIAL

The term "workflow" comes up frequently in the context of collaborative work. A workflow refers to a process or the flow of progress. More simply put, it's all the necessary steps or stages listed in order to reach a result. Not all workflows are necessarily collaborative, but you'll often hear the term used in relation to collaborative remote work.

In practice, adopting a remote-first collaboration mindset within a team that has a hybrid or flexible approach to remote work may mean that location-based employees often end up collaborating as if they were remote too. In other words, in-person employees might be sitting side by side at their desks in a shared office, but given the way they are collaborating with each other and other remote team members, they might as well be sitting in their own living rooms. It can be tough for location-based organizations and employees that don't want to change their ways to accommodate remote work. But it's the best way forward if the organization wants to have a successful remote work culture and keep remote employees for the long term.

Get Rid of Assumptions

The assumption that remote work is "work, but online" is wrong and misguided. Equally, assuming that remote collaboration is "collaboration, but online" is also incorrect. Remote collaboration is different because, when done right, it starts with zero assumptions and builds a totally new understanding of what it means to get work done as a group. Here's an example. In the location-based-work way of thinking, teams might ask, "How frequently do we need to meet to make sure everyone knows what everyone else is doing?" There's an assumption that the team needs to meet. In remote work, the question might become "Do we need to know what everyone else is working on, and if so, what's the best way to do it?"

When you adopt a remote collaboration mindset, you can think clearly about what you want to accomplish with a group and the best way to accomplish it together within the constraints of remote work. When you get rid of assumptions about what collaboration ought to be, then you're more open to what it could be.

Tools Used in Remote Collaboration

Getting rid of assumptions about what collaboration should be is an important first step. After that, it helps to know what tools are available to support different kinds of remote collaboration so you have a better idea of what's possible.

There are hundreds, if not thousands, of collaboration apps on the market. Some are generic and flexible, meaning they aren't built specifically for any type of business or project and you can customize them to do what you want them to do. Others are highly specific to an industry, such as real estate, or to a type of work, such as programming.

Broadly speaking, there are seven types of collaboration apps that can show you new possibilities for how to collaborate remotely:

- Team messaging apps
- Video conferencing software
- Work management or workflow management software
- Collaborative office apps
- Project management software
- Visual collaboration apps
- Industry- or job-specific collaboration apps

TEAM MESSAGING APPS

Team messaging apps, such as Slack and Microsoft Teams, are group messaging platforms. You use them to text chat with other people in your organization, and sometimes external partners as well, both directly and in groups. Many organizations use team messaging for internal daily communication instead of email.

VIDEO CONFERENCING SOFTWARE

Video conferencing software, such as Zoom and Google Meet, lets two or more people have video and audio calls, as well as share what's on their screens and sometimes add ideas to a virtual whiteboard together. Remote teams typically use them for meetings.

WORK/WORKFLOW MANAGEMENT SOFTWARE

Work management or workflow management software are apps that let teams write down the work that they are doing, details about each task (assignee, deadline, progress, etc.), and track it through a workflow. Additionally, these apps also allow other team members to see that activity and, in some cases, manage it too.

Imagine an article making its way through the publication process before fancy apps and computers. That article is in a folder, and attached to the outside is an assignment sheet with the names of all the people who have to interact with it before publication (senior editor, copyeditor, art department), what they have to do (edit for substance, edit for errors, design artwork for the piece), and their deadline for passing it on to the next person. That's what work management apps do, but they put the information online so that everyone can see it at any time.

Some work management apps are essentially to-do lists, but with collaboration features built into them. Others are much more complex and can overlap with another category of collaboration apps, project management software, depending on how you use them. Some examples of work management apps are Asana, Trello, Basecamp, Todoist, and Airtable.

COLLABORATIVE OFFICE APPS

Collaborative office apps are standard office apps, such as Microsoft Word or Google Slides, that include options to collaborate. Most office apps today have collaboration capabilities built into them. "Collaboration" in this context means synchronous and asynchronous coauthoring, as well as the ability to leave integrated comments on a file and make suggested edits that the lead author can accept, reject, or modify.

PROJECT MANAGEMENT SOFTWARE

Project management software is similar to work management software, with a few key distinctions. First, project management software is for projects. Projects are sets of work with a start date, end date, and deliverable date. Building a house is a project. Answering support emails is better classified as ongoing work. Projects that require project management software tend to be very complex and therefore require a lot of planning.

Think about how a construction team can cut lumber at the same time that they pour a foundation, but they can't install windows until the building's basic structure is in place. Now imagine a company that builds fifty houses in a year and has to stagger when the foundation-pouring crew works on each site as well as when the window installers should go to each site. What happens when it rains and the schedule for pouring foundations is suddenly two days late? Everyone else's schedule has to shift too.

Project management apps handle this kind of work. They make it easy to see who is supposed to do what at a given time and how to adjust the entire schedule (or find a way to make up for it) if one piece falls out of place.

VISUAL COLLABORATION APPS

Visual collaboration apps include apps for brainstorming, like virtual whiteboards, as well as apps for creating diagrams, flowcharts, and other designs. As with office apps, you can collaborate in these apps both synchronously and asynchronously.

INDUSTRY- OR JOB-SPECIFIC COLLABORATION APPS

Industry- or job-specific collaboration apps are ones built for a specific use. For example, sales teams typically use customer relationship management (CRM) software, which tracks the dates when they reach out to potential customers, what they discuss when they reach them, and any next steps that someone on the team should take. There are collaboration apps specific to programmers, educators, marketers, screenwriters, and many other job functions and industries.

Evaluating Synchronous versus Asynchronous Collaboration

If you've only ever worked a location-based job, you might not have ever encountered the idea of synchronous (in real time) versus asynchronous (not in real time) collaboration. When talking about collaboration, you could use "simultaneous" instead of "synchronous" because they both mean two or more people collaborating with one another at the same time.

Synchronous Collaboration Is Precious in Remote Work

In location-based work, it's easy to take synchronous collaboration for granted. If everyone works in an open-plan office together, you can spin around in your chair and ask a colleague for help or input. You can call an impromptu team huddle to review everyone's progress with their current task. You can tap on someone's shoulder and ask for their feedback. Some people valorize these spur-of-the-moment acts of collaboration by overlooking the fact that they have the regrettable tendency to be highly interruptive.

In remote work, synchronous collaboration almost always needs to be planned in advance. When you have employees spread across time zones, you can't send everyone on your team a text message saying "Let's get on a video call right now" and expect them to show up. People could be enjoying their personal time or asleep or working on something that requires high focus and ignoring their messages until it's finished. Remote work values worker autonomy to the extent that one person can't expect their colleagues to drop what they're doing to do something else.

As a result, synchronous collaboration tends to be rarer in remote work than location-based work. And when something is rare, people assign a high value to it. Synchronous collaboration is precious and should be treated that way. In other words, when you can get people together to simultaneously collaborate, you want to make the most of every minute.

When a team or organization develops the mentality of treasuring synchronous collaboration, it becomes more intentional. People plan ahead by answering questions that will make the time spent together as productive as possible:

- What do we want to accomplish by working together in real time?
- How will we do it?
- How much of what we need to do must happen in real time and how much can we do asynchronously?

> **ALERT**
>
> Developing good collaboration practices in an organization is really hard, regardless of whether employees are remote or on-site. Even when it's done well, it still might not be ideal. Keep in mind that you can always make collaboration better, but you'll never make it perfect.

Async Everything

Because synchronous collaboration is rare and precious in remote work, asynchronous collaboration is abundant and bandied about. You might hear people say "default to async" or "assume async." In other words, when thinking about and planning how to get work done with others, assume it will be asynchronous and use asynchronous methods by default.

Some examples of asynchronous collaboration are asking people for comments on a design and giving them three days to do it, coauthoring a document over time, having many people contribute ideas to a brainstorming file when it's convenient for them, and so forth.

The beautiful thing about asynchronous collaboration is that by its nature, there's always a record of it. Something is written down or there's a finished product with a version history showing how it came to be. Having and sharing those records by making them accessible to employees fits with the remote work values of overcommunicating and being transparent.

For asynchronous collaboration to work smoothly, however, everyone must agree to some rules of engagement, which will be covered later.

Adopting a Capture-and-Share Mentality

The more people work and collaborate asynchronously, the more they're likely to adopt a capture-and-share mentality, which means making a record of your work and sharing it with others. If it sounds like yet another manifestation of internal transparency and overcommunicating, that's because it is.

Capture Your Work

Capturing work often happens by default. A lot of work that can be done remotely produces evidence: documents, reports, lines of code, graphics, and so on. As noted earlier, asynchronous collaboration by its nature creates a record. Another simple example of capturing work is to take notes in a meeting (or record the meeting if it's a video call).

Work management apps and other collaboration apps help teams capture information too. For example, when a team decides on a particular workflow or procedure, it can be captured in the team's work management app by creating a template. It might not be necessary to explain how the team came to every little decision about each step, but the final result can be captured and saved in the app.

Thinking and decision-making that happen only in people's heads or orally take a little more effort to capture, however. Workers need to purposefully write down that kind of information to capture it.

ESSENTIAL

For decades, organizations have struggled to capture and share institutional knowledge, which is information about how an organization runs because it typically resides only in people's heads. Remote-first organizations may not do it perfectly, but they are much more proactive about capturing and sharing institutional knowledge.

Share Your Work

The "share" part of the capture-and-share approach is making your work and records available to others. Because sharing is built into so many remote collaboration apps from the start, it's a fairly passive process much of the time.

As mentioned, work management apps have sharing built into them, as do office collaboration apps. Shared servers and cloud storage systems, such as Dropbox, Google Drive, and OneDrive, operate in tandem with collaborative office documents. Those servers and storage systems make it easy to give everyone in an organization access to files they need.

QUESTION

If I share all my files, isn't that an invasion of my privacy?
No, not if you're employed full-time. Employees sometimes forget that their employer owns all the equipment they use: computers, email systems—everything. It's even easier to forget when you live and work in the same place. If you can, keep separate devices for work and personal use.

As an employee, you may be encouraged or required to store your work in one of these shared spaces where your colleagues and bosses can get to it at any time. That access is good not only for remote collaboration but also for business continuity. If something happens to you that puts you on unexpected leave, someone in the organization knows where to find all your work in progress.

Shared servers and storage systems are also efficient at locking down sensitive information, such as HR files and invoices, by putting them into folders with restricted access. In fact, many collaboration tools offer permission levels and settings that restrict who can access the information or to what degree they can alter it. For example, in some systems, you can give people the power to edit files but not delete them. For all the tools your remote team uses to share work, get to know the permission levels and settings they offer.

Problems with the Capture-and-Share Approach

While there are numerous benefits to maintaining internal transparency and overcommunicating by capturing and sharing information, there are also some disadvantages and common pain points. Key among them is that getting into the habit of capturing and sharing information creates a deluge of it. A common problem in remote work is feeling overwhelmed by information. Your organization's leadership team and your boss may encourage you to consume as much of it as you can. Frankly, that's not realistic; you have to pick and choose. Otherwise, you risk having to process so much information about work that you have no time to do the job you were hired to do. It can take time to figure out a strategy for selecting the right information to consume. It's not about knowing everything; it's about knowing the right things.

Another problem that crops up with information sharing is deciding how much to share. When you undershare, people don't have sufficient information. When you overshare by providing unnecessary details, it adds to the information deluge. It takes time and practice, and it's okay to get it wrong sometimes. You can improve at it by paying attention to how much detail other people share or by asking for feedback. You might have a good idea what level of detail your teammates need from information you share, but you might not know who else consumes it and what they do with it. Just ask.

You can also be selective in how and when you decide to alert people to some information that's available to them. For example, even though all your files may be accessible to your boss at any time, you don't have to tell your boss every time you create a new file. In some cases, it makes sense to not publicize your work until it's ready for sharing. You might not want input on a project until you've decided for yourself how it should go. Getting feedback and input too early can sometimes muddle your own thinking. It can also create a dynamic where people suggest additions to your project that you already had in mind but simply haven't put in yet. Whenever you have work that isn't yet in a good stage to receive feedback, you can say so. Or, better yet, say nothing at all, and people probably won't notice that it's available to them.

Another problem has to do with duplication and version control. Sharing information and overcommunicating can result in duplication, and that's often intentional. You want to make information available in more than one place. But doing so opens you up to version control issues. For example, your team has a workflow in a template in your work management app. Your team also has a shared document that captures that same workflow and explains how and why you all use it. One day after a team discussion about the workflow, you make a change to the template. But you have forgotten entirely that the other documentation even exists, so it remains unchanged. Now your team has conflicting information. When it happens with one or two documents or for one or two details, it's usually not a big deal. Over many years, however, the problem compounds. It's a known problem, and there isn't a fail-safe solution at this time.

Setting Boundaries and Rules for Collaboration

How people collaborate and communicate dictates the team dynamic and its stability. When people collaborate in an intentional way by being conscientious of how they do it, there's more harmony and ease in the team's interactions. In remote work, the best way to make sure your team will collaborate effectively and productively is for everyone to establish and agree upon some basic rules and boundaries.

Agree on Shorthand Replies

One very simple and somewhat fun rule of collaboration is to use reacji for shorthand. Reacji, you might recall, are emoji used as a reaction to someone's message or post. Your team or organization can decide what kind of shorthand responses make sense and which reacji to use for them.

For example, if someone asks a question in a team messaging app and you want to indicate that you've read the question and are looking up the answer, you might use the reacji of two eyeballs looking left or right. If a manager posts an important message and asks everyone to read it, it could be agreed-upon shorthand to add a check mark reacji to indicate you have.

You can even use reacji in a more impromptu way to quickly survey people. Perhaps you have three design options in a visual collaboration board. You can write a comment in that system and ask people to reply with their favorite by using the reacji 1, 2, or 3; or if the designs are three distinct colors, use reacji that match up with the same colors.

Using reacji as shorthand is an excellent example of a way to communicate and collaborate with a team that's clear, effective, and concise.

Determine Expected Response Times

Remote teams use, as you know, a lot of different systems to collaborate and communicate. Another set of rules you and your teammates can create is to have expected response times for different systems.

Team messaging apps tend to be the tool for day-to-day communication, so they might have the shortest expected time of response. If you ask a question there to a whole group (say, everyone on the research and development team) and you wait for the first available person to answer, perhaps the agreed-upon response time is within six hours. If you ask a question in your team's work management app directed at a specific person, maybe the expected response time increases to twenty-four hours. With email, you might extend the expected time to be three days. Those are all examples, but the point is, it can vary based on the type of collaboration app, who uses it, where those people are located, and so forth.

Having an expected response time also helps people sort work effectively. When your team messaging app has a short response time, you check it more frequently. If email has a longer response time, you don't need to spend as much time in that app. Plus, when everyone takes a moment to think about the true urgency of a question, you become more attuned to prioritizing effectively.

One hitch in asynchronous remote work is that you can get blocked from making progress on a task while you wait for a reply, a document, or an approval. To combat that issue, some remote-first companies have a policy of defaulting to action, mentioned previously. "Default to action" means if you can make a reasonable guess or assumption about how to proceed before you receive whatever it is you're waiting on, go ahead and move forward. Most of the time, your work won't be in vain. Occasionally, however, you might end up having to undo a day's worth of work. It's a business risk, but if it plays to your advantage most of the time, then it's probably worthwhile.

Only "default to action" if your organization or team agrees that it's a rule you should follow.

Know *When* to Collaborate

In remote work, *when* you choose to collaborate can affect your work–personal life boundaries. In organizations with a strong, positive, supportive remote work culture, *when* you work really should not matter at all. In reality, that's not always the case.

What happens when you and your boss work in the same time zone and you get notifications that she's updating files at 6:30 p.m. and sending questions to you at 6:45 p.m.? It can start to feel like you really should respond right away. Or what happens when you open your team messaging app and email at 7:45 a.m. and see several messages from your teammates that you've only just received in the last hour? Do you start to feel pressure to respond right away and push off everything you had planned to do that morning?

In remote work, you should be able to work when it suits you, but sometimes teams get lax about overcommunicating this. As a result, people instead pick up on cues and subtle pressure to work with more urgency. This is especially true when pressure is high in the organization, such as when a big project is due or a launch is coming. The next thing you know, everyone is having knee-jerk reactions rather than sticking to their rules of collaboration and taking their time to respond.

One trick that helps is to work when you need to but hold off on sending messages, emails, or notifications until it looks like an appropriate time to respond from your teammate's point of view. For example, some email programs and team messaging apps have a feature called Schedule Send that lets you choose a time and date when your message should go out. That way, you can write the message when it suits you, but send it later. Additionally, with some collaboration, you can work off-line and then upload or sync your changes later. In both of those examples, you get to work at times that are best for you while your colleagues assume you're working standard business hours.

Another helpful trick is to minimize notifications of changes that other people make in collaboration apps. If you're expecting a colleague to make changes to a shared Google Doc and that person will let you know when they're done by updating the team's work management app, then you don't also need to receive notifications from Google. Go ahead and turn those notifications off. These are just added noise and can send you the wrong signal about how to work.

Beware of Collaboration Burnout

In the business world, "collaboration" has become something of a darling term. It has a positive connotation. Business leaders push for more collaboration, even when they don't have a firm grasp on what it means or how it happens.

FACT

According to a 2016 *Harvard Business Review* article, collaboration activities had increased by more than 50 percent since the mid-1990s, but the value of those efforts was lopsided. Twenty to 35 percent of value-added collaborations came from only 3–5 percent of employees.

When employees and managers feel pressure to collaborate, or at least to be seen collaborating, it can result in collaboration burnout, especially among top performers. What happens is that someone who collaborates well and adds value to collaborative efforts earns a reputation for it. As this reputation develops, demand for this person increases, and everyone wants to pull this employee into their meetings and brainstorming sessions. Everyone wants this person to weigh in on their work or project. After a while, the highly valued contributor sees their time to focus on core work get sucked away. That's how collaboration burnout happens.

FACT

Work and research by Renee Cullinan, summarized in a 2018 *Harvard Business Review* article, suggests that women disproportionately feel the burden of collaboration compared to men. The reasons are tough to untangle and are a mix of social and psychological effects, though much of it comes down to expectations of women to "care for the collective."

To prevent collaboration burnout, protect your time by gently pushing back if you're invited to too many meetings or collaboration sessions that aren't central to your work. Suggest alternative, asynchronous ways to offer your advice, input, or reflections that are less time-consuming. That way, you will still have time to do whatever high-focus solo work is central to your job.

Case Study: MURAL's Meeting Rule: No Agenda Means It's Optional

At MURAL, a company that makes visual collaboration software of the same name, there's a rule that if a meeting doesn't have an agenda, it's optional. If you want to get people together, synchronously, for a meeting, then you must have a clear purpose and objective for the meeting that you share in advance with your invitees.

Mariano Suarez-Battan, CEO and founder of MURAL, says he thinks deeply about what a team can accomplish only when the members are together, such as generating ideas and connecting with one another on an emotional level. Those types of moments should happen in meetings.

Information sharing, however, doesn't need to be a meeting. For informative meetings, he says, "we try to do as much as possible that's prerecorded, either with documents or videos"; in other words, they use asynchronous collaboration methods instead. The time spent together is precious, he adds, not only because the all-remote team has to coordinate time zones, but also because meetings drain people's energy and have a financial cost. The company's rule that "if there's no agenda, the meeting's optional" makes everyone think twice about how they choose to collaborate and nudges them to use more remote-friendly tools and methods. The result is better remote collaboration and fewer meetings.

Maintaining Living Documents and Documentation

Living documents and documentation are files that contain some of that institutional knowledge mentioned previously. They are the procedures, philosophies, and rules of an organization. What makes them alive, so to speak, is that they are never considered finished. Rather, they are fluid and updated frequently.

While living documents aren't unique to remote work, they tend to be more important to remote workers than location-dependent workers. In location-dependent work, you can always find someone to answer your questions when you have them. Remote workers, however, must be able to look up information independently as much as possible. They can't rely on another person being available at all hours to answer their questions.

Living documents contain answers to many questions remote workers have about work and how to do it. To keep living documents alive, people need to collaborate to update them regularly, which means someone has to decide who will update these documents and how often. How do you do that?

Don't Let It Be a Free-for-All

Collaboration software often comes with permission settings, which let you (or the app administrator) determine who can access, edit, and delete content. The granularity of these settings varies by app.

For simplicity's sake, or sometimes as a result of an app having limited options, it's common that everyone on a team or in an organization will have full read-write capabilities to some set of files. In other words, everyone has the same level of unrestricted editing power, which is typically the case with living documents.

If everyone has read-write access and makes changes to files when they notice something needs updating, the files can get messy. Even if the collaboration system keeps a good record of the change history, wading through dozens of edits to select the right one is a nightmare and creates needless work. So you really need a more formalized solution.

Nominate Someone or Let People Volunteer

One solution is to nominate someone, or encourage a few people to volunteer, to be the keeper(s) of a particular file. This method works well for certain kinds of institutional knowledge that fall to one person. If you're hired to start a company newsletter, for example, you might be the only person who knows how to write and send it. Therefore, it would make sense that you become the keeper of the living documentation about the newsletter.

Write down everything someone would need to know about the newsletter, including screenshots, links, and notes that explain "why" when relevant. Make sure you save the file somewhere that's accessible to everyone on your team or open the permission settings for access.

> **ALERT**
>
> If you're hired to create a new product or procedure, or revamp an existing one, you can easily win over your manager and teammates by documenting it. For procedures, document them in such a way that anyone else could read the documentation and do the job for you. Remote workers who do this task without being asked are highly valued.

Set a Rotating Schedule

Another solution is to have people take turns updating living documents. There could be a rotating schedule so that once a month, someone from the team or organization looks over the files to make sure they're up-to-date.

One benefit of this solution is that if someone leaves the team, the document isn't suddenly abandoned, which would be the case if only one person ever updated it. However, this solution doesn't work for procedures and information that are well known to only a select few.

Working Together on Visual Materials

Collaborating on written files is much different than collaborating on visual material. Designers and artists have a language and learned sensibility for discussing their work that people in other job roles often lack. Designers joke about getting completely useless feedback like "Make it sexier," or "I don't like that color." Collaborating on visual materials when you don't have the knowledge or words to do it well is challenging.

Equally challenging is having to create professional-looking visual assets when neither you nor anyone on your team is a designer.

There are some collaboration apps and tools that make it much easier to discuss or create visual material (although they won't improve your artistic sensibilities).

Markup Tools

Markup tools are tools inside an app that let you draw on top of another file. They can be as simple as an arrow that you lay on top of an image to point to something or sticky notes that you write on and stick next to the part of the image you're referencing.

Diagramming, Flowchart, and Mind-Mapping Apps

When you need to make a professional-looking graphic and have no artistic talent or training, you can turn to an app that includes premade objects, shapes, and templates for whatever purpose you have in mind. If you and a remote colleague need to draw mock-ups of a mobile app design, for example, or an org chart, you can use a diagramming and flowchart app such as Lucidchart or Draw.io to work on it together, whether synchronously or asynchronously. Unlike illustration or vector graphic apps, where you have to draw the images you need, diagramming and flowchart apps give you a library of premade objects that you simply drag and drop onto a page and put them where you want them.

Mind-mapping apps are similar, although they often include tools that let you import information from another app. If you and your team want to brainstorm ideas related to all your clients, for example, you could use a mind-mapping app to first import a list of all your clients. Two examples are Mindomo and MindMeister.

Other Visual Collaboration Software

Visual collaboration software is a somewhat new and quickly growing category. There are some interesting and innovative apps that empower remote teams to collaborate in new ways. For example, some of them offer templates that are designed to facilitate team-building exercises or ice-breaker activities. Others let you and your team turn a brainstorming board into an interactive presentation.

It's good to know these apps exist because they can broaden your idea of what kinds of collaborations are possible in remote work.

CHAPTER 7

Remote Work Is Reshaping Meetings

The remote work movement may be the influential force on the future of meetings. Remote-first organizations treat meetings as precious commodities. The "Does this need to be a meeting?" question comes up often. While some location-based businesses may have asked that question before, it's simply more meaningful in a remote environment, where meeting time is literally hard to come by. That said, remote work done poorly is an absolute disaster for meetings and thus remote teams. Developing the right attitude, strategies, and rules about meetings in remote work is vital.

It's Time to Rethink Meetings

For years, meetings have been one of the top pain points for knowledge workers, usually second to email. Employees find them distracting and interruptive to their core work. Location-based businesses haven't done nearly enough to reexamine their need for meetings or changed why and how they hold them. But remote-first organizations have.

A positive remote work environment places high value on employee autonomy. Additionally, it places value on letting people work uninterrupted on tasks that require high focus, as those tasks typically have the greatest return for the business. Those tasks are the core work of any individual.

The way that an organization shows it values worker autonomy and demonstrates that it will protect people's ability to work uninterrupted is by not making too many demands on their time. And when an organization does need to do so, it should be beneficial. In other words, if you're going to call a meeting, it had better be a good one.

This is all a long way of saying that when an organization is very careful in how it handles meetings, it shows respect for employees and their work.

In a perfect remote work world, meetings are rare, precious, and effective. In a more typical world, however, remote teams do struggle from time to time to live their values when it comes to meetings. Under the worst circumstances in remote work, meetings lose their aura of being highly valued treasures; instead of being rare, they are constant. They don't have a clear purpose, waste peoples' time, and drain everyone's energy. Having unnecessary meetings leads to high levels of burnout, sometimes higher than what's seen in location-dependent work.

It's so important to get meetings right in remote work, or to at least consistently make the effort to do so.

Meetings Are a Last Resort

In remote work, some say that meetings should be a last resort, not the first option. People should only meet when they have no other way to accomplish whatever it is they need to accomplish.

Remote workers can become skilled at collaborating digitally and asynchronously in a variety of ways, as shown in the previous chapter. When you know what tools are available and you practice using them, you may see different means for achieving an end.

For example, if a team needs to brainstorm ideas, discuss them as a group, and decide on the top three ideas, how much of that needs to take place in a meeting? Many teams would default to holding a one-hour meeting, and maybe if someone put five minutes of thought into it, write an agenda asking people to arrive with ideas for the brainstorming part.

But here's a different way to do it:

1. Create a shared document or visual collaboration board where everyone adds their ideas asynchronously when the time is right for them to work on that task, which also gives people time to think through their ideas without pressure.
2. Next, decide whether your team hashes out ideas better in real time or asynchronously. Depending on the answer, either schedule a fifteen-minute meeting or give everyone a deadline for adding their comments and having a discussion in the same app where the brainstorm took place.
3. Lastly, everyone on the team can take their time to think about the discussion and vote on their favorite ideas in the shared file.

By deciding what you need to accomplish and thinking of alternative ways to do it that are not rooted in meetings, you can often come up with ways to work that are better and more effective. Everyone has time to think about the best way to contribute, and they can do it when it's right for them, rather than at an arbitrary meeting time, which might interrupt other work.

Meeting Time Is Precious

When remote teams are distributed globally, finding meeting times is challenging. Coordinating schedules and time zones can make it difficult to find a meeting time and date that works for everyone you want to invite to a meeting. But there are additional reasons that meeting time should be seen as precious.

For one, meetings are expensive. For full-time salaried employees, every minute spent in a meeting has a literal cost. Take your annual salary and divide it up into weeks, days, and hours if you want to know how much it costs your employer for you to be in a meeting. For freelancers, contractors, and some self-employed types, some meetings are billable to the client, and other meetings are not billable, meaning you (the freelancer or contractor) have to configure the cost of the meeting into your rates and fees or look at meeting time as a sunk cost. Plus, how much time did everyone spend coordinating the meeting time? Those costs add up.

Remember, too, that all the time you spend in meetings is time not spent doing your core work. That's a cost to the employer for sure, but there may also be a cost to your morale if you feel like your time isn't respected. It's one thing to have a tight deadline but another to have six hours of meetings eating away at the time you should be using to hit a tight deadline.

ESSENTIAL

Finding a time when people across time zones can meet is tough, but apps such as Doodle and Rally make it easier. These apps let you create a poll with suggested times and dates for a meeting. When your invitees open the poll, the suggestions appear in their local time zones. Everyone votes on which times work for them so you can find the best option.

How Long Should a Meeting Be?

If meetings are a last resort and meeting time is precious, then meetings should be only as long as they need to be to achieve the desired outcome or end.

The only exception, and it's more of a semantic one, is for postmortems or retrospectives. Those kinds of meetings should be as long as they need to be (rather than *only* as long as they need to be).

Social expectations can sometimes make it seem like it's rude if you don't give a person a half hour or full hour for a meeting. Really, it's just the opposite. If you accomplish what you need in eighteen minutes, it's respectful to end the meeting early and give that person their time back. In remote work, almost all your meetings are virtual, so no one has to plan their whole day or week around traveling to you. Some industries may still have expectations for what's considered a respectful amount of time for a meeting, but if you want to make remote work function, everyone really needs to shift toward the idea that a meeting doesn't need to last a set amount of time.

Cut off any meeting that gets stuck or where the participants seem drained and unable to contribute effectively. If a meeting is going badly (about thirty to forty minutes in is a good time to make the call), end the meeting and consider collaborating in a different way or resuming at a later time.

What Are Meetings Best For?

Another way to think differently about meetings is to consider what can happen only in meetings and no other way, or what happens best in meetings compared with any other way.

Meetings do have a value and a place in business. The only way to use meetings strategically and sparingly is to know what that value is.

Perhaps most importantly, in a remote environment, meetings are the primary way to connect emotionally. True connection happens by seeing other people's facial expressions and body language, and by hearing the tone of their voices. Getting to know people in a meeting with all these additional cues helps you better understand the same people in their written communication. This richer understanding further develops and builds the more you communicate with them through other channels.

Meetings also give you and your colleagues an opportunity to express an emotional status change. In written communication, you can tell someone that you're feeling additional stress or are burned-out or nervous or ill, but seeing and hearing someone express the same thing in a video call can give it additional meaning.

In addition, meetings are very effective when a team needs to generate or evaluate ideas or information quickly. Certainly, asynchronous collaboration works just as well, if not better, when there's no time pressure. When you need to work quickly, however, a real-time meeting is one of your best solutions.

Prepare for Meetings and Make the Most of Them

In learning to think differently about meetings, remote employees need to prepare for meetings and make the most of the time spent together in them. This goes not only for the person who arranges and plans the meeting but also for the participants.

Before any meeting, read the agenda, look through any materials provided in advance, and compose your thoughts. Every meeting should have a purpose, and for every meeting you attend, you should have a purpose for being there. What do you want to get out of the meeting? Why are you attending? If you aren't sure, ask the person who planned the meeting.

Your purpose could be clear and concrete, such as to receive specific details that will inform your work or find out what additional tasks you need to do. Other times, you might attend meetings for soft knowledge, such as to observe how different parties interact or to clarify someone's position or how they're feeling about a project. Depending on your personality type, you might attend meetings because you feel more energized and reassured when you have regular video-based contact with some of your colleagues. Those are all perfectly valid reasons.

Why Meeting Burnout Is High for Remote Teams

When meetings are handled poorly in remote work, they can lead to meeting burnout that's just as high, if not higher, than in location-based work.

As mentioned, meetings take up time, and they take away time from core work. They interrupt your ability to have long stretches of high-focus time. Most people find meetings drain their energy, especially when they're expected to attend multiple meetings per day or per week.

Video Preview Windows Add Extra Stress

For many people, online meetings are even more draining than in-person meetings because of the hypervigilance created by being on camera.

When you see a preview window of your own face (which you can hide, by the way), it makes you more aware of your own presence. "How are other people seeing me and interpreting my facial expressions? Can they hear my child or pet in the background? Should I mute?" For people who are affected by the camera in this way, being in virtual meetings is extra stressful and leaves them feeling depleted.

There Are Fewer Barriers to Invite Participants

Additionally, in remote work, there are fewer barriers to entry for someone to attend a meeting. In location-based work, clients and outside partners might have to travel to you for a meeting, or vice versa. In offices, there are limited conference rooms and limited seats at the table. Virtual meetings don't have those same limitations. In remote work environments where people are not attuned to how precious meetings should be, it's easy to invite everyone who's even tangentially related to the purpose of the meeting. When someone receives an invitation to a meeting, especially if it's from a superior, it's assumed that their attendance is mandatory. Moreover, the more you get invited to meetings that aren't important, the more you resent being invited in the first place.

When these forces combine, they create an environment where meetings aren't effective or valuable, hardly anyone enjoys them, and meeting burnout is high.

Do You Need to Attend Every Meeting?

Some remote work advocates say that if you're feeling stressed and burned-out in a remote job, push back on meetings. The reason? Meetings tend to be the culprit of unhappiness in remote work, and when they are, you can usually get out of some of them.

But there are ways you can push back on some meeting invitations.

How Will You Participate?

If a questionable meeting invitation lands in your inbox, ask yourself and the meeting coordinator whether you need to be in attendance. If the answer is yes, ask the meeting coordinator for a clear agenda and what you will be expected to contribute. The best-case scenario is that the meeting coordinator will provide you with information and resources that allow you to adequately prepare for the meeting and thus help it run efficiently and wrap up quickly. If the meeting coordinator doesn't have an agenda and can't say for sure how you might contribute, then you might be able to push back and again question why you need to be included.

How Else Might You Contribute?

In discussing with a meeting coordinator whether you'll be expected to participate in an upcoming meeting, you might glean that there's another way for you to contribute without actually participating in a synchronous meeting. For example, before the meeting, can you share information using an asynchronous collaborative app? Or can you prepare something that another colleague in attendance can present on your behalf?

If a meeting is supposedly informational for you, ask the meeting coordinator to record a video of the call and send it to you after. That way, you still get all the information from the meeting and can review it at a time that's right for you. Plus, you can skip forward through any greetings and chitchat. You might even watch the video on 1.5x speed or listen while doing something else that doesn't require your full attention.

Overcommunicate Your Meeting Burnout

Another way to push back on meetings is to overcommunicate the fact that you are experiencing meeting burnout. Provide feedback to your teammates, manager, or supervisor, whoever is most appropriate.

Remember to shape your feedback so that it's constructive. Explain the conditions that are creating this sense of meeting burnout. Is it because you have too many meetings or because the meetings are too long or poorly organized? See if anyone else on your team feels the same way. Also share what you could or would be doing with the time you're spending preparing for meetings, showing up to them, and recovering from them.

> **ALERT**
>
> If you're burning out on meetings and you're invited to optional meetings, absolutely skip them. Don't feel guilty for it. If an "optional" meeting turns out not really to be optional, you have bigger issues of communication and trust to deal with.

Ask to skip some of the usual check-in meetings or make them less frequent. There is no rule that a one-on-one meeting must be weekly. If it works for both you and your manager to make it every other week or once a month instead, try it and see if that helps ease the feeling of meeting burnout.

Standing or Stand-Up Meetings, All-Hands Meetings, and One-on-Ones

In remote work (and at some location-dependent workplaces too), there are three types of meetings that are extremely common: standing or stand-up meetings, all-hands (town hall) meetings, and one-on-ones.

These meetings are usually recurring, meaning they take place on a regular, repeating schedule, such as once a week or quarterly. There are other regularly scheduled meetings, such as annual or quarterly planning meetings or strategy meetings, but those are specific to people in certain roles or at certain levels in the company, whereas the other three apply to everyone in a remote organization.

Standing or Stand-Up Meetings

The standing meeting or stand-up meeting is a team meeting usually held once a week. Some people say it's called a "standing meeting" because it's always at the same date and time (a standing time), and some people call it a "stand-up meeting" because it's supposed to be short enough that most people can literally stand through this brief team huddle.

Most teams like to hold their standing meetings either at the beginning of the week or the end of the week because they can think and talk about the week ahead or reflect on the week that's ending. Some teams have a standing meeting twice a week so they can do both.

A standing meeting should not be for rattling off information that everyone on the team can easily find elsewhere, such as the list of tasks assigned to you in the team's work management app or project management app. It's better to use this time to explain or discuss something that might not be transparent to everyone, such as why a task is blocked or whether you're unsure what your top priority should be.

Additionally, standing team meetings are a great opportunity to repeat (overcommunicate) important information that might otherwise be forgotten, such as planned time off or other upcoming events.

All-Hands Meetings

An all-hands meeting, or town hall meeting, is an organization-wide meeting. Everyone is invited. Depending on the size of the organization and frequency of these meetings, everyone may or may not be expected to attend. The more infrequent they are, the more likely it is that attendance is mandatory, or at least "highly encouraged."

In small organizations, all-hands meetings could be once a week or once a month. In large organizations, twice a year or annually is more the norm.

For small organizations that have frequent all-hands meetings, and where attendance probably isn't mandatory for each one, be on the lookout for special instances, such as annual or twice-yearly updates on the organization's finances, strategy, or structure. A good leadership team with a remote-first approach will let you know when there's an all-hands meeting you're highly encouraged to attend.

One-on-Ones

A one-on-one meeting is a recurring meeting between an employee and their manager or boss. They're typically held once a week, although once every other week may do too. One-on-ones go by many names (one-to-one, 1:1, 1-2-1), but the idea is generally the same. It's a standard check-in meeting between employee and manager meant to be driven by the employee, though some managers might bring an agenda as well.

The one-on-one is your opportunity to talk about what you need, what you want, questions you have, and so forth. While you can mention the status of your work, the one-on-one shouldn't be only about daily tasks. You might, however, discuss how your work contributes to the team and its goals, or whether your daily tasks are in line with your intended career projection and how you see yourself advancing in the organization.

While there is no rule about how long or short a one-on-one meeting should be (it should be only as long as it needs to be, right?), speak up if they seem to go on too long or end before you've addressed all your issues. It benefits no one if the meeting drags on for no reason or if you feel rushed through it.

> **ESSENTIAL**
>
> One-on-ones are your time. Come prepared with items to discuss. If you don't have an agenda, your manager will likely take control of the meeting and ask about your role, what's most difficult in your job, how you see your career progressing, and other similar topics. It's best to plan for your one-on-ones so you can make the most of them.

TAKE INITIATIVE IN ONE-ON-ONES WITH YOUR MANAGER

When you are new to a remote job, the first few weeks of one-on-ones may cover rudimentary matters, such as making sure you filed all the necessary paperwork for payroll and learning who's who in the organization. Over time, however, you should take the reins of the meeting and use the time to address anything on your mind.

In some employee-manager relationships, the one-on-one meeting might have a bilateral agenda, meaning your manager will come prepared with points to discuss too. That's fine. Certainly, your manager should use the one-on-one to give you feedback. Be careful, however, to not let your manager run every meeting from start to finish. It's your time. If your manager disagrees on that point, have an open conversation about what is the intended purpose of the meeting and ask when *is* your time for discussing matters that are important to you.

DEVELOP THE RELATIONSHIP

The primary way employees and managers get to know one another is through one-on-one meetings. These meetings let you connect and, over time, build trust. Because of this important human connection, it's advisable to use video for most of your one-on-one meetings. That way, you get to know one another's tone of voice, facial expressions, body language, and sense of humor. Those little additional bits of information help you build an idea of who this person is.

Because they take place frequently and between only two people, one-on-ones are informal. There is, and should be, a little time for chitchat. You can share as much or as little personal information as you feel comfortable doing.

If you're not comfortable sharing about your personal life or you are neurodivergent in a way that you need to plan for this type of talk, steer the chitchat toward something you can talk about easily or don't mind discussing. Some safe and easy topics are a book you read or a television show you like. It's fine to have firm boundaries, but it also helps facilitate the one-on-one if you know in advance what you are comfortable discussing.

ASK FOR WHAT YOU NEED

The one-on-one is also the time to ask for anything you need. These can be practical items, such as office equipment, software, or training, or to be paired with a mentor. Your needs can also take the form of asking for help and guidance, such as advice for adjusting to a remote environment or working with a particular colleague.

Use the one-on-one to get answers to questions you have too. They may include clarifying an objective or task, learning more about what's expected of your role, or digging deeper into the organization's mission statement and purpose.

DISCUSS WHAT YOU WANT

Another use of the one-on-one is to discuss what you want to get out of your role and career. You might not bring it up in every meeting, but from time to time you should clue in your manager as to where you'd like to see yourself develop and progress. If you're keen to take on new responsibilities or get a promotion, for example, mention it and ask what you would need to do to get there.

Over the course of your one-on-one meetings, your manager will likely check in to review your goals, see what kind of progress you've made, and, when necessary, update your goals. If your manager doesn't check in on your wants and desires for your career progression, make a point to bring them up occasionally. Your manager should be investing in your success and career development. If they're not, you might have to spell it out for them by taking initiative in this area.

QUESTION

Is behavioral feedback appropriate in a one-on-one meeting?
Opinions vary, but providing feedback on unwanted behavior, such as yelling or using offensive language, is probably better addressed in a separate meeting, possibly alongside another party, such as an HR representative. Behavioral feedback can sour a meeting and make it difficult to accomplish anything else. Consider keeping it separate.

GIVE AND RECEIVE FEEDBACK

The one-on-one meeting is an opportune time to give and receive feedback that isn't urgent. (Some feedback needs to be given immediately to prevent problems from recurring or escalating.) A good manager will give you consistent, relevant feedback in your one-on-ones. It should include praise and recognition as well as constructive feedback meant to help you improve at your job.

You should be proactive in giving your manager feedback during one-on-ones too. Remember to include positive feedback, and make it relevant. When they give you a useful suggestion or insight, tell them why and how it helped. If they contributed to you making progress toward or reaching a goal, share that fact. Include constructive feedback as well, such as mentioning anything that isn't working and why. For example, if you feel your one-on-ones are too frequent or take up too much time, say so and explain how you could use that time more effectively for your job. Be open to listening to your manager's interpretation of the feedback as well, as they may see it differently.

ALERT

Excellent managers are rare. Unfortunately, not all managers are cut out for their roles, and not all receive adequate training. In remote work, the problem is compounded because managers need additional skills to manage remotely. Give your manager clear feedback about what they do that helps you and hinders you. It helps them do their job better.

PERFORMANCE REVIEWS

Every so often, perhaps quarterly or annually, expect to have a special one-on-one with your manager for your performance review.

There are any number of formats for a performance review these days, and yours may come with a template and a name. Whatever the case, the performance review is typically when the employee receives summary feedback, promotions, and salary increases. The performance review is not the only time you should discuss those three items, however.

By the time the performance review rolls around, the decision about whether to promote you or increase your salary may already have been made. If you're vying for a title change, promotion, or raise, make sure you discuss this multiple times in your one-on-ones well before the performance review. Talk with your manager about creating a plan to achieve your goals, or discuss what reasonable expectations you should or shouldn't have. That way, by the time the performance review comes, your manager is clear on what you hope to get, and you're clear on what's possible.

Tips That Make Meetings Relevant, Useful, and Accessible to All

Much of the analysis and advice related to meetings in a remote work setting are applicable in location-dependent work too. There are two key differences, however. First, some of the challenges related to meetings are heightened in remote settings. Second, remote-first organizations are in a unique position to rethink how they want to get work done and how to do it well, and that includes tearing down old paradigms about meetings and starting with a fresh idea of what they should be.

If you want to be a part of the remote work movement and see it succeed, you'll do well to let go of all your old attitudes and beliefs about meetings.

Meeting Time Is Precious: Treat It That Way

It bears repeating: Meeting time is precious because synchronous communication time is precious. When everyone on a remote team treats it that way, it shows respect for everyone else.

Limiting meetings and making the most of the time spent in meetings signals an understanding that everyone on the team has important work to do and that they do it best when they have autonomy over their time, and you can't have true autonomy over your time if you're constantly expected to drop everything to show up to a meeting.

Does It Need to Be a Meeting?

Before scheduling any meeting, the meeting coordinator must question whether it needs to be a meeting. What is the purpose and desired outcome, and can those ends be achieved through some other means: a shared collaborative document, an email, an asynchronous brainstorming session on a collaborative whiteboard, a prerecorded video?

Also ask whether everything you want to accomplish must be done in the meeting. Can some information sharing or brainstorming happen before the actual meeting? When you offer people multiple ways to participate and contribute, it opens up possibilities for people who aren't at their best in real-time meetings. Some people feel more confident expressing their ideas when they have time to think them through and decide how best to share them. For others, there might be a practical reason they work better in asynchronous platforms, such as having a stutter or a difference in abilities.

Save the meeting part for collaboration that can happen no other way or for collaboration that happens best in meetings, like connecting and evaluating ideas quickly.

Have an Agenda, Purpose, and Objectives

How many meetings have you attended that had no agenda? It is all too common for people to call a meeting without being clear on what they want to accomplish. In remote work, where meeting burnout can happen fast and meeting time should be treated as a precious commodity, there's no excuse for calling a meeting without first telling everyone explicitly what it's for.

When someone writes a meeting agenda, it demonstrates that they've spent at least a moment or two clarifying for themselves the purpose of the meeting and its objectives. If you're invited to a meeting that doesn't include an agenda, ask for one.

Integral to the idea that a meeting should have an agenda, purpose, and objectives is the matter of following up if the purpose or any of the objectives were not met during the meeting itself. If anyone is expected to take additional action as a result of the meeting, that information should be recorded in some way, such as writing it in meeting notes or creating tasks in a collaborative work management app.

Make Meetings Only As Long As They Need to Be

When a meeting has reached its conclusion, end it. There is no need to let a meeting drag on longer than it needs to be. When there is no natural end, a good rule of thumb is to end a meeting after about thirty to forty minutes.

For meetings that are meant to build ongoing relationships and foster connections, it can help to have a planned end time. In deciding how long those meetings should be, keep in mind that people often need additional time to prepare for a meeting and then recover after it. If you want to dedicate an hour, schedule the meeting for forty to forty-five minutes. That leaves you (and the invitees) room on either side for pre-meeting setup and post-meeting reflection.

Capture and Share the Meeting

Capture and share meetings so that anyone who could not attend can get the relevant information from a meeting. One way to capture a meeting is to record video of it, but that's not the only way, and sometimes it's not the most effective.

Keeping meeting notes in a shared document is a succinct method for capturing and sharing key ideas from some meetings. Collaborative brainstorming and whiteboarding apps give you another option, and you can use them before, during, and after a meeting. For meetings where slideshows are used, make the slides available, perhaps alongside notes explaining any additional details that were discussed.

For all-hands meetings (town halls), consider recording them as video so anyone who could not attend has the option to get the full experience later.

Look for Closed-Captioning and Transcription Options

Some video calling and meeting apps include options for real-time closed-captioning and transcription options for calls that you record. Both are valuable tools in making meetings more accessible.

Closed-captioning, for instance, helps people who are deaf or hard of hearing, or whose primary language is something other than what's being used in the meeting. It also comes in handy for anyone in a noisy environment or who is having technical issues with their audio.

Transcription services are sometimes available for recorded meetings. This means sometime after a call ends, you receive a typed electronic document of everything said in a meeting. Again, this makes the information from the meeting more accessible to more people. It also allows everyone to search a transcript for keywords rather than rewatch a video to find important information.

Remember That Meetings Have Costs

To reiterate one final point about how to make meetings relevant and useful, always remember that meetings have costs. They have a cost in time, money, and human energy, and they are expensive (another reason they should be rare).

To keep people operating at their best and to keep work flowing smoothly, keep in mind what a meeting costs.

CHAPTER 8

Maintaining Productivity and Avoiding Distractions

In remote work, it's absolutely possible to be more productive than if you were in a shared workspace, but your productivity will look very different. Although remote work has its benefits, including the ability to choose where you work and create a workstation that's tailored to your liking, it also comes with a slew of distractions. If you're new to remote work, many of them may be surprises. Thankfully, you can learn to manage some distractions and deploy techniques to help you focus and get your best work done.

Don't Compare Your Productivity

For people who are new to remote work and have prior experience at a location-dependent job in a similar role, it's very tempting to compare how you work remotely to how you worked at your previous job site. Don't.

You will have days when you don't feel productive. You may have streaks when you don't feel like you're making progress or pulling your weight. There could be times when distractions are happening nearby, such as construction work or a screaming child, that make it feel like you have done nothing for hours and hours. That's okay.

Conversely, you might have days or weeks at a time when all you do is work. You respond to emails before breakfast. You finish an assignment late at night. You pick up your laptop Saturday morning to check that something you did earlier in the week is correct. That's okay, too, as long as your work isn't always that way. If it is, you should have some honest conversations with your manager and reflect on whether it's your habits or the job demands that need to change.

Remote Conditions Are Different

The conditions of working remotely are categorically different from the conditions of in-person work. Remote work comes with all new distractions and interruptions. Some are specific to your personal life, some are related to your environment, and some come from the fact that you simply have more freedom when you aren't working under the watchful eyes of other colleagues and managers. It may seem like these distractions cause your personal productivity to take a serious hit, but that may not be the case at all.

The issue is that distractions at home or in other remote workspaces are rarely work related, making every moment that you're not actively "working" more apparent. Conversely, interruptions and distractions in a shared workplace *feel like work*, regardless of whether they are, so they're less apparent.

When you're new to remote work after working at a location-dependent job, it's easy to forget (or to have never recognized in the first place) how much your work time was broken up when you were in a shared work environment, like an office. Location-based work is filled with interruptions!

In-person meetings, face-to-face questions and discussions, chitchat in break rooms and restrooms, fire and safety drills, celebrations for someone's birthday and another person's baby shower, and so on. Many of those interruptions still *feel* like work, whereas interruptions in a remote environment *feel* like personal time not spent working.

Cut yourself some slack and don't compare them. It's not useful.

Hyperaware When Remote

When you're new to remote work, it's incredibly easy to be hyperaware of all these new freedoms, distractions, and interruptions. What you don't want to do is interrogate yourself with questions like "Would I be doing *this* if I were in an office or on a job site?" Your "this" could be anything from showering at 11:00 a.m. to taking time away from work to clean up after a leaky pipe. No, you wouldn't be doing those things if you were at a shared work location, but you're not.

ALERT

When you're new to remote work, you have to cut yourself a lot of slack by not overanalyzing your perceived productivity. It can take months or years to get a realistic sense of how productive you are in a remote work environment because it's so different from being at a job site.

Similarly, being new to remote work can lead you to become hyperaware of how much work you get done and when. If you've had experience in a location-based job before, you probably weren't nearly so cognizant of your productivity. So if you don't know how productive or unproductive you were before, how could you possibly compare your productivity now to that past time?

Accept the fact that such comparisons don't serve you. Remote work is different. Try to see it as a fresh start.

Productivity *Can Be* Higher for Remote Workers

Here's some encouraging news: Productivity can be higher among remote workers than location-based workers. It's hard to say with certainty that all remote workers are always demonstrably more productive than workers at fixed job sites, but there's decent research to support that it does happen.

Why is it not definite? Many jobs that can be done remotely don't come with easily quantifiable metrics. In other words, it's hard to measure productivity. Often, researchers use "perceived productivity" as a measurement instead, which essentially means how productive a worker reports feeling. It's not a terrible measurement, but it's not hard data. When researchers do use perceived productivity as a measurement, it helps to look at a meta-analysis of research (a study of many studies) to look for more conclusive trends.

ALERT

Research and data on remote workers' productivity during the COVID-19 pandemic are not especially insightful. The overwhelming majority of people working remotely at that time didn't opt in to it; they were forced. Plus, so many other conditions were different, such as children schooling remotely, that the period from early 2020 to late 2021 is an anomaly.

Every so often, however, an organization or researcher can collect hard data on remote workers and measure their productivity against a location-based control group. In those cases, it's important to keep in mind what kind of workers were involved in the study and other details that are specific to their situation. Your circumstances probably don't line up perfectly with the people in those studies, so take their results with a grain of salt when thinking about how they might apply to you.

A META-ANALYSIS OF REMOTE WORKERS' PRODUCTIVITY

One meta-analysis of remote workers published in 2007 looked at forty-six studies that included more than twelve thousand workers. It found that remote work (called "telecommuting" at the time) increased job satisfaction and worker performance (productivity), while decreasing turnover intent (quitting) and role stress.

The researchers suggest that these positive outcomes are at least partially related to the fact that when employees work remotely, they feel they have more autonomy.

MORE PRODUCTIVE AT HOME: SUPPORT CALL WORKERS

Here's an example of hard data from a company that experimented with a work-from-home option. A 16,000-employee Chinese travel website and agency, Ctrip, wanted to see if it could save money on office space and furniture by letting some employees who answer support calls work remotely. So the company set up an experiment. It asked for volunteers who would be willing to work from home for nine months. About half of the volunteers were randomly chosen to do so. The rest of the team was a control group who stayed in the office.

The results, summarized neatly in *Harvard Business Review* (and more formally presented in *The Quarterly Journal of Economics*) found that the remote workers were about 13 percent more productive than staff in the office. The remote group also reported being happier, and they quit at half the rate of the others. The productivity gains alone amounted to nearly one extra workday a week.

The company believes about one-third of the productivity increase had to do with having fewer distractions and a quieter environment. The rest of the boost came from working a little longer (remote workers started on time because they never had problems with weather or commuting), taking shorter breaks, and taking fewer sick days.

In the Ctrip case, the company had initially intended to save money on real estate and office costs by letting employees work from home. In the end, Ctrip estimates it spent $1,900 less per employee over the nine months. But that figure turned out to be minuscule compared to the productivity gains.

There are four important points to note about this particular case.

1. The experiment lasted nine months. That's enough time for people to experience both the positive and negative moments associated with working from home.
2. The employees volunteered to work remotely. They opted in to it rather than being forced.
3. The increase in productivity was steady throughout the whole nine months, indicating it wasn't front-loaded due to an initial burst of enthusiasm.
4. Employees answering support calls are a specific kind of worker doing a specific type of task. Their productivity is easy to measure. Their need to collaborate is relatively low. And working in a central office with other call center workers is noisy because they overhear one another, whereas taking calls from home is likely much more tranquil.

While the results of this study are certainly encouraging, it's good to keep these details in mind and recognize that the results won't apply equally to other workers and types of work.

Measuring Productivity in New Ways

Now you know that you can potentially be more productive in a remote environment but that you shouldn't compare your remote productivity too much to how you used to work in a location-based job.

You also know that remote work isn't just "work" shoehorned into an online environment. It's different, and the way to make remote work great is to recognize it for what it is and think in new ways about how to operate best in this different setting.

One of the ways you should think differently is how you measure and view productivity.

Output over Hours

A trend among remote-first organizations is to value output over hours. The idea is that for many job roles, an organization pays a worker to do a particular job, not sit in a chair for eight hours a day. Therefore, the employer shouldn't care too much if employees get their jobs done in forty hours per week or thirty.

That doesn't mean you have full autonomy over which hours you work, usually. As mentioned, most full-time employees stick to some kind of schedule to make themselves available at reliable times and to be a dependable teammate. You need to reply to questions that other people have and pass along work in a reasonable time frame, as well as meet other expectations. That said, if you can get your job done in six hours per day instead of eight, why shouldn't you?

ALERT

The output-over-hours mentality doesn't apply to workers whose work is measured in time, of course. Think of customer service representatives, for example, who respond to support emails or take phone calls during set hours. Some jobs are still managed and measured by hours.

When organizations focus on output over hours, it forces them to be clear about employee roles and expectations. If you're being paid to do a job, not sit in a chair, then the organization has to tell you clearly what that job entails and how it plans to measure your success. For you as the worker, that's extremely beneficial. It's much easier to do your job thoroughly and well when you know what it is.

It's a Marathon, Not a Sprint

Remote-first organizations that fully embrace the idea of doing business differently and better often focus on success in the long term. There is value in letting employees work thoughtfully and intentionally, even if it means giving up speed. To put it another way, work is a marathon, not a sprint. This concept plays out in at least two ways.

The first way is employee retention. An organization that takes its time to find good employees, interview and hire them, onboard them, and train them knows how expensive it is to go through that process. For that reason, organizations want to minimize how often they do it. That is to say, once they hire you, they want to keep you.

Remember, remote jobs are highly competitive and often come with generous benefits to sweeten the deal so that organizations attract the very best talent. After that top talent (that's you) joins the team, they become an investment to the organization. To retain people, organizations have to keep them happy. To keep workers happy, employers cannot burn them out and treat them as replaceable.

FACT

Burnout and work-related stress are related but different. People experience stress all the time and have ways of coping with it. A little stress can be beneficial. In high quantities, it's detrimental. People can work through stress (whether they should is another question). Burnout is more akin to exhaustion. Burnout is never beneficial, and you can't work through it.

The second way is employee burnout. For you, the employee, your work should be a marathon and not a sprint to prevent burnout, increase your engagement, and help you be that valuable investment that the organization wants. Preventing burnout is a two-way street. Your job shouldn't make it impossible for you to get your work done in a reasonable amount of time, and you have to not push yourself too hard in the wrong ways as well.

So when you think of your productivity, don't just think about what you can get done in an hour or a day. How can you be productive consistently for the entire month or year? How do you need to work differently to sustain high-quality output over many years? The answer is by pacing yourself. Certainly, there may be times when deadlines are tight or you have to work extra hard to quell unexpected problems, but that should be the exception, not the norm.

It's not any different for freelancers, independent contractors, and other self-employed types. Your career is a multidecade journey. When you don't have a workplace to go to and there's no social pressure to show up or leave at a certain time, it can be enticing to pour all your energy into your business and work extremely long hours. It does not benefit you in the long run, however, to burn out quickly or young. It's not about what you can get done right now. It's about how you grow your profession or business consistently over many years.

Setting New Expectations for Distractions

There's no way to predict all the distractions that surface while working remotely. They vary tremendously based on your circumstances, location, personality, and other factors. Regardless, there are a lot of them!

Some distractions are temporary. Some are permanent. Some are easier to manage than others.

Home Distractions

Distractions in the home range from pets, children, family members, and roommates to housework and needed home repairs.

Pets, young children, and home repairs often create distractions that you can't predict. With adolescent and teenage children, as well as adult family members and roommates, you can talk and negotiate with them, but they still may create distractions that are difficult to manage.

Housework is incredibly distracting for some people and not even an issue for others. Can you ignore a pile of dishes in the sink, a countertop covered in crumbs, or floors that need sweeping? You might not know until you're faced with a difficult work project and you don't feel like doing it.

> **FACT**
>
> In 2020 a survey of more than two thousand people, Statista found the top five distractions for remote workers were social media, smartphones, binge-watching, kids, and gaming. Rounding out the list were news media, pets, online shopping, and partners. Interestingly, only about half of those distractions are specific to remote work.

For people who live alone and are more extroverted than introverted, a unique distraction can be that the home is too quiet and too isolated. Extroverts feel energized when they are around other people. That means their energy and ability to focus can wane as the day goes on without sufficient contact.

Food can also be a home distraction. Working next to a fully stocked kitchen can be as much of a distraction as it is a wonderful perk of remote work, depending on your relationship to food.

Outside and Environmental Distractions

Outside and environmental distractions are completely out of your control. They include loud construction and landscaping, your neighbors and their noisy activities, and deliveries and repair people arriving at your home or remote work location.

Depending on where in the world you are, you may also have intermittent electricity or Internet outages, as well as weather and environmental events that cause similar disturbances. If you decide to live and work in Southeast Asia, for example, you might want to first read up on when the monsoon season is before committing to projects on tight deadlines.

Self-Interruptions

Self-interruptions are distractions that originate in your mind. They include the desire to check messages on your phone, respond to personal emails, look at sports scores, and so forth. Self-interruptions usually start with a thought that you may or may not act on (e.g., "I just remembered that I have to call to schedule a medical appointment before 4:00 p.m."). Whether you stop what you're doing to make the call is up to you. Regardless, the thought interrupted you.

Some self-interruptions are in fact short breaks that can be beneficial. Microbreaks or workplace Internet leisure breaks, for example, help restore your mental capacity to continue working. Other self-interruptions are personal necessities, the things you need to get done during business hours. As long as they don't get out of hand, these kinds of interruptions in the workplace are okay and usually expected, and they aren't terribly different in remote work compared with location-based work.

Tips for Dealing with In-Home Distractions

As mentioned, some in-home distractions are manageable and some are not. As any good therapist would say, you cannot control what happens, but you can control your response to it.

Overcommunicate with People in Your Space

Some of the more manageable in-home distractions include those created by other adults who share your space, such as partners and roommates, and older children.

Use the same overcommunication tactics that you use in your remote job to talk about what you need and what you consider distracting. Be open to listening to what the other person needs too. For example, if you're trying to create quiet time to focus on work during the same hours that your roommate exercises loudly and uses the blender to make a recovery shake, you both have to discuss what you want and why, and then look for a compromise. Maybe you both need to wear headphones during exercise time, and you can agree on a set time when the roommate uses the blender so you at least know when that noise is coming and can plan for it.

While you can talk and negotiate with older children, they're still children who don't have all the skills yet to know in advance what they need in order to plan accordingly. Again, talk about what you need and come up with rules or guidelines. Perhaps you tell your kids that when they come home from school, they shouldn't interrupt you until a certain time unless there's an emergency. If there's something urgent but not an emergency, they can text you or knock softly on your door. Build in conditions that acknowledge and show respect for everyone's needs, and know that even with guidelines in place it's not always going to work out perfectly.

Work with or Around Young Children and Pets

Young children and pets are less predictable and less open to frank discussion and negotiations. So the burden falls on you to figure out what's causing them to distract you and how to cope.

The best you can do is identify the problem from both your perspective and theirs. Is your pet or child interrupting you or distracting you at a predictable time of day or for a predictable reason? If so, you can try to plan around it. Feed the cat early; take the dog on a longer midday walk; switch up your work hours when your baby's nap time starts to fluctuate. If you have another person who helps with caregiving responsibilities, share the full picture of the problem with them so they know not only how to help but why. They may have other ideas for solutions that aren't apparent to you.

ESSENTIAL

You know what's best for your kids and how to keep them busy. In a remote job, you might have to pull out the high-value treats, like video games and extra screen time, more often than you would have previously. Come up with guidelines that work for your family and also let you focus on your career. Both are important.

Rarely will you find a perfect way to curb distractions caused by young children and pets, but you can identify the problem and then work with it or around it.

Write Down Distracting Household Chores

Some people have no problem ignoring housework to do their jobs, and others find it incredibly distracting.

When you're new to working from home, it might seem like you can squeeze in a chore here and a chore there to stay on top of both the housework and your paid work. It's not nearly as easy as it sounds, however. If you're fastidious about housework, you might already know that it never ends. There's always something else to clean.

The following is a good strategy for housework:

1. Write down what needs to be done when it pops into your mind
2. Prioritize the tasks you can reasonably do in a short amount of time
3. Plan when you will do them

You'll see this same method for dealing with interruptive thoughts crop up a few more times in this chapter. It's a tried-and-true technique that works in many different contexts.

If you struggle with having plentiful amounts of food within reach, you can try this same strategy for planning meals and snacks too. Write down what you want to eat and when you'll eat it so that you get the idea out of your head for now and promise yourself a reward at your next break or when the workday ends.

Here's how it looks in practice: Rather than have a knee-jerk reaction to the thought of needing to empty the drain catch in the kitchen sink (or grab a snack), write it down in your to-do list or on a sheet of paper. Keep your notes nearby so that you can write down other chores and interruptive thoughts that come to mind, such as taking out the trash and running a load of laundry. When you have a break, decide which chores can fit into the rest of the day's schedule. You can knock out the kitchen drain catch right now and put in a load of laundry at lunchtime. At the end of lunch, the laundry will be ready to hang or put into the dryer. Folding the laundry? That can wait until the evening or tomorrow. The trash? If it's not urgent, save it for later, or ask someone else in your household to do it.

> **ALERT**
>
> Many of the distractions around you will become less distracting as time goes on, but it could take a year or more. Additionally, some distractions are easier or harder to deal with at different times of the year. Be patient and don't be too hard on yourself. It takes time to develop a remote work lifestyle.

The longer you work from home, the more easily you'll recognize which chores fit into a workday routine and which ones to avoid because they lead you down a rabbit hole. For example, taking out the trash might lead you to want to wipe out the bin, sweep the floor around the bin, and empty the recycling containers too. Before you know it, one quick chore turns into a half hour of tidying up. If you're afraid of getting distracted further, simply write down the task and note that you'll do it after the workday ends or on one of your free days.

Embrace Your Flexibility

As much as you don't want to get distracted by housework or other in-home distractions when you're trying to work, remember to embrace your flexibility in having a remote job. Take care of what needs to get done. The most important things don't have to wait. It's not unreasonable to take a five-minute break to move laundry from the washer to the dryer.

Embrace your flexibility for the things you love too. If you enjoy baking bread, and remote work makes it possible for you to punch down some dough and pop it in the oven while you're working, have at it. Taking time for what makes you happy is important to your well-being and stamina. Remember, it's a marathon, not a sprint.

Tips for Managing Outside and Environmental Distractions

When you work remotely, it might seem like every day is roadwork construction day, or lawn mower day, or car horn–honking day. Outside and environmental distractions cause huge disturbances when you're trying to concentrate on work, and it's worse if you have a lot of video calls scheduled or do any kind of audio or video recording as part of your job.

Similarly to dealing with other distractions that you cannot control, the best you can do is plan for some of these interruptions and work with them or around them.

For Repetitive Outdoor Distractions, Leave

The first time landscaping noise interrupts your work, it's annoying. By the third or fourth time, write down when it happens and look for a pattern. Does your neighbor blow leaves every Wednesday afternoon? If so, plan around it. Go work from a different location during the days and times you anticipate the noise.

You can use the same trick for other street noise, as long as you adapt the habit according to the pattern. For example, neighborhood construction might be ongoing for weeks. See if you can find out how long it will last (look online or call your local authority's information line). If it's neighbors doing construction, talk to them and ask about the timeline. Then plan to work somewhere else during the worst parts of it. For example, go to a café, coworking space, or a friend's house where you can work. You might even tie in an incentive for yourself to make it more enjoyable. Splurge on breakfast while you work from a café, for example, or shift your hours to work later to accommodate the interruption and treat yourself after to make up for the inconvenience by getting a manicure or having a beer.

Reset after Other Unexpected Interruptions

If you primarily work out of your home, you might soon have a new appreciation for how often service workers come by to deliver packages, read the water meter, fix the cable lines near your home, and so forth. For these types of distractions—the kind that are completely unexpected and relatively short-lived—there's not much you can do to plan for them.

If they take you out of the flow of working, you might have a hard time getting back into it. Give yourself a reset. Try changing something in your immediate environment to signal to your brain and body that you're starting fresh. Move to your secondary work location, put on music, make a cup of tea, or light a candle. Or take a fifteen-minute break and then resume your work.

Weather events and other natural disasters also cause interruptions and distractions, especially when they knock out the power or Internet. Sometimes they're foreseeable, and sometimes they come out of nowhere.

ESSENTIAL

For areas where power outages are frequent, look into buying a universal power supply. It's essentially a giant backup battery. You plug devices into it and then plug it into a standard outlet. It stays charged while delivering a steady flow of electricity to your devices, and when the power cuts, the battery is already in place to keep your devices running uninterrupted.

If you're in for a storm that could potentially cause Internet or power interruptions, save some work off-line if you can (that is, assuming the storm is safe to work through).

Tips for Handling Self-Interruptions and Personal Distractions

Self-interruptions and distractions, such as checking messages or remembering you have to make a doctor's appointment, can seem more difficult to ward off when you work remotely compared with being on a job site. When you don't have the social pressure of other colleagues casually observing what you do, the "right time" to handle personal issues is amorphous.

Just as with being distracted by housework, your best bet is to write down these items when they pop into your head and plan when you'll do them. Planning can be specific, such as adding a task to your to-do list and scheduling a reminder for a particular time. Or planning can be loose, like "on my next break," whenever that may be.

Sometimes, however, you should feel free to embrace the flexibility that remote work provides and take care of interruptive thoughts and tasks in the moment. If you've procrastinated making a medical appointment and it's on your mind right now, go ahead and take care of your personal business. Flexibility is only a perk and privilege of remote work if you make use of it.

The fact is, the conditions of working at home and working in a shared location are different, and they're not comparable. Dwelling on them creates needless stress. Accept that you're in a different environment when working remotely and that you need time to develop a new understanding of what it means to be at work and what a day's work looks like.

Using Sprints to Tackle Difficult Tasks

The most difficult and most important tasks in your job probably require intense focus and stretches of uninterrupted time. You might call these tasks your "core work," "high-focus tasks," or "deep work" (a term largely attributed to Cal Newport, who wrote a book by the same name), or something else. Whatever you call it, it's the tough work that you get paid to do, rather than the work about work. One of the tricks of being productive at work is making time to do that core work and then focusing on it intently.

The remote-first mindset says making time to focus on your core work is a high priority. There are two techniques, which are very similar, that can help you make time for this work and follow through on doing it with intention and focus.

While these techniques are not exclusive to remote work, they are especially relevant in situations where you have a lot of autonomy over how you work and there's no social pressure to be seen sitting in a chair working. For example, they're popular among students who are writing their dissertations, as well as writers, artists, and other solo-working creative types.

The Pomodoro Technique

In the late 1980s, Francesco Cirillo developed the Pomodoro Technique and wrote a book by the same name (*The Pomodoro Technique*) that describes a method for getting high-focus work done. It involves focusing intently on one thing for twenty-five minutes and then taking a short break, usually between two and five minutes long. You repeat this cycle about three more times (meaning you do four focus sessions in total) and then take a longer break.

FACT

Pomodoro means "tomato" in Italian—the name of the technique comes from the tomato-shaped kitchen timer that Cirillo used to measure his work and break intervals. He also says he likes the ticking sound it makes, as it helps him focus. Cirillo now has a free web app with a ticking timer so that you don't have to buy a little tomato.

There's a little more to the technique as Cirillo describes it. Before you start, you need to decide what you're going to work on. The more specific, the better. Also, grab a piece of paper and a pen or have a note-taking or to-do list app handy, because anytime a thought distracts you while you're in a work session, you're supposed to write it down. That way, you can deal with those thoughts during your break, not while you're trying to focus.

Having paper at hand also lets you track how many work-break cycles you've done so that you know when it's time for a longer break.

Focus Sprints

Focus sprints are extraordinarily similar to the Pomodoro Technique, only they don't have a trademarked name and they are less stringent about the length of time for the work interval (focus sprint) and break interval. Otherwise, they use the same concept and procedure: Decide on a task you will do, be clear about what it is, set a timer to work on that task without interruption, and when the timer runs out, take a break.

QUESTION

Exactly how many minutes should I work intently for maximum productivity?
There's no magic number for work and break intervals. If you look for research on the subject, you'll find any answer you want to find. It depends on the task, how you're feeling, and other factors. Experiment and change the number of minutes as needed.

While you should absolutely adjust the length of your sprints and breaks, you don't want your focus sprints to be too long. Part of the technique involves taking a short break before you feel like you need one. Keeping your focus sprints shorter than one hour seems about right for most people.

In addition to Cirillo's app, there are many free apps and browser extensions you can use to time your focus sprints and break intervals. These apps ring to remind you to start and stop, and some of them let you submit a list of websites that you find distracting so that the app can block them when you're in a focus sprint. Strict Workflow and Focus 45 are two examples.

Using Time Blocking to Manage Your Daily or Weekly Schedule

Another way to be productive and focus on your core work is through time blocking. Again, this technique is not exclusive to remote work, but it is especially relevant when you're working alone and learning to manage your time independent of a nine-to-five job clock.

What Is Time Blocking?

Time blocking is exactly what it sounds like. You block off time on your calendar and dedicate it to something. Typically, a daily schedule has time blocked off for appointments and meetings. Time blocking as a technique, however, is like creating a series of appointments that are only for yourself. You quite literally block off chunks of time in your calendar to do whatever it is you need to do.

For example, you might pencil in time for core work from 8:45 a.m. to 9:30 a.m., followed by a planned fifteen-minute break. Then from 9:45 a.m. to 10:15 a.m. you might block off time for catching up on team messages and email. You continue to block off time for as much of the day as you need.

Some people like to plan out a week in advance, scheduling the most important things they need to get done across several days. Whether daily or weekly time blocking is right for you depends on what kind of work you do, what kind of deadlines you have, and how far in advance you like to plan.

What Does Time Blocking Do?

When you start a day's work, how do you decide what you will do and when? Do you know in your head what needs to be done first and then wing it?

Time blocking adds structure to your day. You plan what you will do, when you'll do it, and for how long. It helps you organize, prepare, and set expectations for your work.

Think about attending a conference or a full day of training. At the beginning of the event, you receive a schedule that shows exactly what you'll be doing or what's offered at various times of day. That schedule helps you create expectations for the day and prepare yourself for what's ahead. For example, if you have an hour of programming that sounds boring followed by a one-hour class where you expect to learn a lot of applicable tips and tricks, you're not going to devote all your attention to the boring programming. Instead, you're going to save your energy to soak up the interesting stuff.

When you use time blocking as a technique, you can schedule your day in such a way to alternate between high-focus tasks and more monotonous work so that you never get stuck doing hours and hours of either one continuously. You can also plan your breaks. In remote work, it's not uncommon to see people time blocking for exercise, outdoor activity, and other breaks that are important to their well-being.

ALERT

Be careful how you label your time blocks. In remote work, it's common for teammates to have access to one another's calendars to make scheduling easier. That means everyone can see your time blocks. For anything sensitive, use a generic label, such as "personal commitment."

Additional Advantages of Time Blocking

Time blocking can also help you estimate how long it takes to do tasks. When you first start blocking your time, you'll probably find that most tasks take much longer than you expected, and some take less time. The more you do it, the better your estimates will get.

You'll be wrong about other estimates, too, like how long it takes to prepare for and recover after meetings. You might at first plan to take a five-minute break after a meeting before starting a new task, and over time you realize you need a solid half hour before your brain is ready to jump into something new. As you observe and learn, you'll get better and better at planning.

For time blocking as well as focus sprints and other techniques to keep your productivity high, you don't have to commit to using them every minute of every day, and they aren't mutually exclusive. Try different techniques and then use them when it makes sense.

CHAPTER 9

Establishing a Solid Work-Life Balance

How do you create a lifestyle that's healthy, productive, and happy when you work remotely? The answer is, it takes time. A lot of mental prep work goes into it, and you have to check in on yourself every so often to take stock of what's working and what isn't. Additionally, you have to communicate explicitly and often with all the people in your life because they don't know what you need to succeed unless you tell them. The rewards are worth it, though.

Defining Your "Balance"

How you define your work–personal life balance is ultimately up to you. In a true remote-first environment where work isn't time dependent, you should be able to work whenever you want at whatever hours of the day or night you deem fit. In reality, neither life nor work is amenable to such a chaotic schedule. Most people settle into a routine of choosing the hours when they'll work and sticking more or less to them, diverging from this schedule only when needed. It's often the best solution, as your coworkers and managers have some idea of when you're available, and you'll have some sense of predictability of your own life.

Without firm boundaries for where or when work happens and when personal life happens, one can bleed into the other. Unfortunately for a lot of remote workers, it's the work time that most often bleeds into the personal time, not the other way around.

No One Will Save You from Yourself

Some people say they don't mind when work invades their personal time. They say that they prefer to respond to work messages on their mobile device at any hour of the day, any day of the week, because for them it's easier and less stressful to respond in the moment than to risk forgetting about it the next day. Even in jobs that aren't remote, you might hear people say this about when they're on vacation. By all means, it is a choice you can make.

Many of these same people, however, learn over the years that there is no real payoff to letting work interrupt their personal time. They would have been just fine responding to messages during work hours, even if sometimes they forgot. Plus, in responding to work during their nonwork time, they never fully feel like they have a life outside of work. Again, in the long run, it can be a damaging relationship.

There's a saying: "The company will never love you back." Remote workers who are dedicated to their jobs need to hear it more than just about anyone. In remote work, no one is going to stop you from responding to messages at 10:00 p.m. or recognize you for going above and beyond for doing so because your hours are set by you. It's really and truly up to you and no one else to define your work–personal life balance. Your colleagues and managers should give you the liberty to do your work whenever you want. So if you're hoping that someone will swoop in to say, "We see you're going above and beyond, but for your own sake, don't, because it's not good for your well-being," well, don't. No one is going to save you from yourself. Be careful about it from the moment you start working remotely.

You Can Prioritize Family and Health

There are situations in which you very well may need to work unusual hours to get your job done. Parents with new children (after taking parental leave) may find the first few months back at work don't lend themselves to the old schedule. Similarly, people with other caregiving responsibilities may find their routine gets interrupted when circumstances change, such as the health of the person being cared for. Even your own health circumstances could change in such a way that makes working at odd hours more convenient.

Remote work can accommodate these needs and fluctuating conditions. Being able to prioritize your family and your health without worrying about being at work during specified hours is an incredible benefit of having a remote job.

ALERT

Even though remote work is fairly accommodating to changing health and caregiving conditions, if you find yourself needing time off, consider making use of the Family and Medical Leave Act. It's a law that protects US employees from losing their job while taking unpaid leave for illness and care responsibilities, including births and adoptions.

Working Flexibly Behind the Scenes

Sometimes when working flexibly, like late at night or on the weekends, you don't want your colleagues or clients to know. The reasons could be personal, such as not wanting to field questions about what's going on that you need to work different hours. Or you might have professional reasons, such as trying to shield other employees from making the incorrect assumption that you're working overtime (which can trigger others to start working overtime, too, or start them worrying that something's wrong at the organization).

It's not hard to mask what hours you're working, but it does take a little forethought.

Work Off-Line, Then Sync Your Changes Later

One way to work any hours you need to without letting other people know is by working off-line and then syncing your changes later (this was mentioned in Chapter 6, but it bears repeating). That way, you get to do your work when you need to, but your teammates will only see activity on your end when you sync your changes.

There's not much to it. Save the work you need off-line. Put the app into off-line mode or turn off the Wi-Fi on your device. Do your work as needed, and then when it's an appropriate hour to look like you're working, reconnect your device to the Internet and sync your work.

This trick works best with apps and other collaboration tools that offer an off-line mode. It also works best at times of day when you're likely to be the only person working on a collaborative file. Otherwise, you may have a co-editing conflict; some apps help you resolve them neatly, but for other apps it's a bit of a pain.

ALERT

Before using any off-line tricks, run a test so you know for sure that they work and how. Even better, download a copy of your work once you've finished just in case something goes wrong in the syncing process.

Schedule Messages to Send During Business Hours

Similarly to working off-line and syncing your changes later, you can also write responses to emails and messages at whatever time you need and schedule to send them at an appropriate time.

Some email programs have a Scheduled Send feature (it might go by another name in some apps) built right into them. Others offer it as a plug-in, meaning you have to install the feature from a third party. A few team messaging apps, such as Slack, also include this feature that allows messages to be sent at scheduled times.

If your email and messaging apps don't have this feature, an alternative solution is to type up your responses to messages in a separate word processing or note-taking app, and when you're ready for the recipient to receive them, paste them into the appropriate program and send away!

Setting Boundaries to Protect Daily and Weekly Time Off

Preserving your regular time off, which for most full-time remote workers means evenings and weekends, is crucial to your long-term success, wellness, and happiness. Turning yourself away from work can be incredibly difficult when there are no physical boundaries preventing you from dipping back into email, messages, documents, and so forth.

Rest Allows You to Stay Productive

Resting and taking time away from work are the only ways to let your mind and body refresh so that you can once again be productive when you get back to it. You're not doing yourself or your job any favors by giving up your leisure time to continue working. Remember, your career is a marathon, not a sprint.

Not working during your time off benefits you, although you don't necessarily have to shut your mind off from work completely, according to research by Kevin J. Eschleman and coauthors published in the *Journal of Occupational and Organizational Psychology* in 2014. A study that looked at four ways people recuperate from work—detachment, mastery, control, and relaxation—showed that mentally detaching from work didn't significantly improve people's job performance (productivity, essentially) as rated by themselves or their colleagues. The other three forms of recuperation did. To briefly explain them, (1) mastery means developing a skill, such as playing a musical instrument, (2) control means having agency over what you choose to do in your free time, as opposed to having obligations, and (3) relaxation simply means relaxing, as defined by the person doing it because what's relaxing for you might not be relaxing to someone else.

Self-Discipline and the Clock

So how do you set boundaries with yourself so that you don't let work creep into the rest of your life?

A lot of it comes down to self-discipline and being vigilant about watching the clock. It takes willpower and, quite frankly, a little bit of self-confidence to decide you've done enough for the day or week and simply turn off your work persona. It's hard, but you can add cues to help.

Setting a rough schedule for yourself, as mentioned, helps guide you toward a routine of stopping work at a certain time of day. The clock isn't very persuasive on its own, however. You can strengthen the role of the clock by customizing some settings on your computer and apps to draw your attention to quitting time.

For example, most computers have a setting for turning down the blue light that emits from the display. If you want to stop work at 5:30 p.m. every day, enable the blue light shift to happen then. That way, the moment you work later than you had intended, you'll know because your computer screen will suddenly have an orange hue.

FACT

Because computers and mobile phones now all have blue light settings, there's no need to buy and wear special glasses that filter blue light. If you like them, go ahead and wear them, but they aren't necessary if you use the tools already at your disposal.

You can set other time-based reminders, such as automating the do-not-disturb feature in your team messaging app to automatically enable at the end of the day. You'll see a change in status in your profile image in the app, another signal that tips you off that it's time to wrap up and enjoy your nonwork life.

If you have smart home devices, you might set other electronic signals and reminders for your designated quitting time. Have a smart speaker announce the time at 5:30 p.m. each workday, or set your lights to turn on or change color at that same time. By enabling an outside signal, you aren't solely relying on your ability to pay attention to the clock.

Once You're Done, You're Done

Often, the best advice is to not look at work during your free time. This is especially true on weekends or anytime you have a full day or more off work.

Once you're done working, close out apps and websites related to work so you're not tempted to look at them. This goes for mobile apps as well as those on your laptop or desktop computer. Quit them completely, and disable their notifications unless you've agreed to stay on call in case something urgent comes up.

As suggested previously, you may want to keep two computers, one for work and one for personal use, or create two user profiles on the same computer to help you differentiate between work and personal time. If you have two machines, shut down your work computer completely at the end of the workweek. That makes it less tempting to open it up.

Sick Days Are No-Work Days

Working remotely sometimes means you can power through a tickle in the back of your throat, a mild case of indigestion, or a slight headache and do a full day's job. Employers certainly like that fact, but go easy on yourself. When you're sick, you're sick. If you have a full-time job that includes paid time off for illness, take your sick days. They're part of your compensation, and they're available so that you can get well.

For independent workers, it's harder to convince yourself to take a true day off for illness because when you don't work, you don't make money.

Sometimes you can drag yourself through a week of mild sickness while working at about 60 percent of your usual capacity. Is it worth it? Would you have healed sooner if you took a day or two off to sleep and rest? It's hard to say. You have to use your judgment. Overall, just keep in mind that you're allowed a sick day when you need one.

Some health conditions, such as chronic pain caused by arthritis, fibromyalgia, or other conditions, are much more difficult to manage. Taking a full sick day isn't necessarily what's going to help you heal or feel better. Sometimes what you need is a lot of flexibility about when, where, and how you work to make accommodations for yourself to deal with and manage your condition. You can sit, stand, move around, nap, stretch, take medication, or even take an hour away from the desk to get a massage. Sometimes working part-time for a day or two might be a good solution. You might also consider working with a coach who specializes in pain management at work, and if you're employed full-time, ask if this kind of service is covered in your benefits package. Of course, if you need a full day or two off work to physically and mentally recover, you should take it.

Taking Vacation Time, Holidays, and Personal Days

Similarly to protecting your evenings and weekends, your vacation days, holidays, personal days, and other paid time off (for full-time employees at least) are times when you get to enjoy your life, but you're also recovering from work so that you can return to work refreshed and rejuvenated.

ESSENTIAL

Not taking all your time off is tantamount to leaving money on the table. Similar to paid sick leave, your paid time off is part of your compensation. Not only do you deserve time off to enjoy your life and recuperate from work; your employer also financially owes it to you.

Remote work makes it more challenging to take time off and not do any work during that time off. It's tempting to check in on the status of work, see if anyone has questions for you, and otherwise make sure business is running smoothly without you. Fight that temptation!

Managers and Leadership Must Set the Example

How comfortable you feel taking time off and explicitly not doing any work while you're away is largely set by organizational culture. Do other people respond to messages and help out when they're supposedly on vacation? If they don't, you can feel confident leaving work behind.

> **ALERT**
>
> Management and leadership must set a good example for employees in this regard. If during a two-week vacation your boss pops into the team messaging channel four times to check in, that's a sign that the organization expects employees to make themselves available during their time off. See it for the red flag that it is.

If that's your predicament, consider sharing feedback with your manager or leadership team to explain that when they check in or respond to messages on their time off, it makes you feel like you should do the same, rather than actually taking time away from work. They should enjoy their time away from work, and you should too.

Working Vacations and Travels

A unique perk of remote work is that you can take a working vacation if you want. Think of all the times you may have had to travel to attend a wedding or special function, and you didn't really want to use your paid time off for it.

With a remote job, you have the option to travel for special events without burning your vacation days. As long as you can get your work done on a plane or during the hours when you're not required to participate, you can work and travel simultaneously. In that sense, you can use your paid time off more strategically.

Dealing with Unlimited PTO

Offering unlimited paid time off is something of a trend among remote-first organizations. When an organization is trying to figure out how many days off per year to offer to employees around the world, where various laws about paid time off apply, a simple solution is to make it unlimited. This solution is far from simple for employees, however.

Unlimited paid time off is never actually unlimited. If you took off ten days every month, you'd lose your job. Without a target for how many vacation and personal days you *should* take, however, you might take too few, which is bad for you! Time off is important to your well-being, your work–personal life balance, and your ability to be a good worker. And, to reiterate an important point, your time off is part of your compensation, so not taking the time off you deserve is equivalent to leaving money on the table.

There are ways to manage unlimited paid time off effectively. One is to ask someone in HR or leadership the average number of days off employees take per year, and if the number includes national holidays, sick days, and personal days. If they are unable or unwilling to tell you, that's a bad sign.

Another way to manage unlimited time off is to make a quick estimate of the minimum amount of time you should take annually based on standards and averages. Start with national holidays. In the US, many organizations, as well as employees of the federal government, observe certain national holidays (New Year's Day, Memorial Day, Independence Day, and so forth), typically about ten per year. If you live outside the US, go by the standard for your country or use ten days, whichever is higher. Next, for vacation days, entry-level employees in the US often start at ten days per year, which is low by international standards. Fifteen days (three weeks) is not unreasonable, and it might be twenty or higher if you have a few years of experience with the organization. Already, counting national holidays and vacation days together, you're at twenty-five to thirty days off per year, and that's before even factoring in sick time or personal days.

Those numbers are not hard-and-fast rules but rather a quick estimate to give you an idea of a target minimum number of days off you should be taking if you're under an unlimited paid time off policy.

Learning to Take Healthy Breaks

When you aren't in a shared work location, there are no social cues for when people take breaks. In an office or other work site, you see other people stepping out for coffee; you hear them coordinating lunch orders; you smell the afternoon popcorn snack cooking in the microwave. All these cues tell your brain and body that you should take a break too.

In remote work, those cues don't exist (unless you're in a coworking space). Even if you work from home and share that space with other people, whether children or adults, the rhythm of their day and their routines and patterns might feel to you more like interruptions and distractions rather than social pressure to take a break.

Breaks are absolutely necessary for refreshing your brain and body so that you can maintain your stamina throughout the workday. Roughly speaking, there are three types of breaks that you need: long breaks, short breaks, and microbreaks.

Long Breaks

For most remote workers, the long break is the lunch break. This is when you take an hour to yourself—half hour, minimum!—to set work aside, take care of yourself, and rejuvenate so that you have the energy and mental stamina to conquer the second half of your workday.

From time to time, you might need to take care of personal chores during your long break. In general, however, try to enjoy an hour-long break as often as possible. Eat something you like or go for a walk. Getting outdoors and exposing your eyes and body to natural light (even with sun protection) can do wonders to rejuvenate your mind. Exposure to natural sunlight also helps some people sleep at night by syncing up their circadian rhythm a little better to match the setting and rising of the sun. (See Till Roenneberg's book *Internal Time* if you're interested in learning more about sleep, chronobiology, and so-called entrainment to the sun.)

To make sure you take an adequately long break once a day, pay attention to the clock or set a timer. Some productivity apps, such as

RescueTime, include an option to pause them or run a timer while you're on a long break. If you come back to your workstation and see that the hour is not yet up, walk away and do something else until your break is over. Don't shortchange yourself with your long breaks. Take them in full.

Short Breaks

Short breaks of anywhere from about three to fifteen minutes allow your brain to take a rest when you start to feel fatigued. Some people like to plan their breaks so that they intentionally rest before they feel wiped out, although a lot of people treat them in a more ad hoc manner.

A short break is a good time to fix yourself a beverage; adjust the lights, temperature, airflow or other environmental factors; turn music on or off; go to the bathroom; and take care of other short-term needs.

Short breaks can also take place online. There's nothing wrong with looking at your phone or a favorite app, reading a news article, browsing sports scores, checking the weather, and so on. If you use the Pomodoro Technique or focus sprints, you can time these short breaks to prevent yourself from getting sucked in for an unreasonable length of time.

FACT

In a survey of office workers published in 2011 in *New Technology, Work and Employment*, productivity peaked when employees spent about 12 percent of their workday taking short, intermittent breaks by doing something on the Internet for leisure. Taking too few breaks or taking too many breaks resulted in lower productivity, indicating a sweet spot for short breaks.

Microbreaks

Microbreaks are very short breaks, about thirty seconds to a minute long, that help prevent repetitive stress injuries and other problems that result from sitting and staring at a screen for too long. Microbreaks can also be somewhat restorative for your mind.

As you might remember from the section on ergonomics, experts on workplace health and safety would ideally like for people who work seated to stand and move around every twenty minutes. Your optometrist or ophthalmologist may have suggested something similar for your eyes: looking away from your computer screen and focusing on something farther away every twenty minutes or so.

QUESTION

What if I take so many breaks that I don't get enough work done?
Relax. Don't confuse feelings of guilt about taking breaks to poor output. Remote-first organizations care about the work you produce, not the number of breaks you take. Measure and track your output before rushing to any conclusions. If your output is indeed low, use focus sprints to work with more intention and time your breaks.

Moving, stretching, and blinking conscientiously every twenty minutes is an ideal, though perhaps it's a little out of reach for most knowledge workers to achieve. That said, an ideal can still be a goal. How motivated you are to reach this goal may depend on whether you experience any discomfort already, such as an aching back, stiff neck, sore forearms and wrists, or dry eyes.

Break apps can help. They freeze your computer screen for a few seconds at an interval you set, preventing you from continuing to work. A few seconds of screen freeze might be the nudge you need to stand, stretch, and look out the window for a moment.

If you use the Pomodoro Technique or focus sprints, you might build movement into those breaks, even if they're longer than one minute.

Another trick you can try to encourage yourself to move more frequently—and this one may sound a little goofy—is to keep a large cup of water within arm's reach and force yourself to finish it once an hour. That way, you'll get up more often to refill it and use the bathroom.

If the water-drinking tactic sounds ridiculous, just try to stand up, look out the window, roll your neck, and give your body a few good stretches at least once an hour.

Finessing Your Routines for Work-Life Balance

In time, you'll likely fall into a workday rhythm: wake up, do your morning routine, start work, take a break, work a little more, eat lunch and go for a walk, get back to work, and so on.

Your routine for working remotely is not fixed. You can change it and improve it at any time. Creating the right conditions to work and live is an ongoing process, and no one ever said you had to nail it on the first try.

> **ALERT**
>
> If you find something about your routine isn't working or you're unhappy, you do have the power to make changes. Yes, change is hard, but it's not impossible. You might also want to change up your routine to prevent boredom or unhappiness before they set in.

Think about finessing your routines to make them better—not "perfect" or "amazing," but better.

Make an Effort to Try Something New

If all is going smoothly with your remote work situation, change something small in your routine every so often to either try a new habit or technique, or simply to mix up the sounds, smells, visual stimuli, and other things in your surroundings.

Try techniques you've never used before. Change the time when you eat lunch. Sit outside during a short break without any electronic devices. Work in a timed focus sprint or start your day by time blocking your calendar. You won't know if you can make your routine better if you never try new things. The worst that could happen is you don't like it, you waste a few minutes, and you go back to your old routine the next day.

Getting Used to Eating

Figuring out and finessing your routine for eating when you work remotely comes remarkably easy to some and is a perpetual struggle for others. Deciding what to eat, when to eat, whether to throw something together quickly or take time to cook, and whether to snack can be incredibly challenging in remote work because the day can feel so unstructured.

If this is a pain point, try different strategies. Prepare lunch for yourself in advance, and then eat that lunch at a set time. Or make several lunches at the start of the week to avoid making a decision about what to eat each day.

Another tactic is to buy premade frozen or refrigerated meals or meal kits and eat one of those on your long break. Similarly to making a meal in advance, it removes or significantly reduces the decision-making process about what to eat.

How you manage food and eating in a remote work setting is extremely personal. Try a variety of tactics until you land on something that is useful and helps you take care of yourself at the same time.

Identify the Rut

When something feels amiss or you're unhappy in your daily routine, the hardest part is often identifying the cause. Maybe your work starts to feel monotonous. Is it the work that's the problem or your stamina? Is your stamina low because you're not getting enough sleep, or taking insufficient breaks and working for too long at a time, or not getting enough physical activity? Figuring out the problem isn't simple. Sometimes you need to work through potential sources of the problem using trial and error.

> **FACT**
>
> Realizing you're in a rut can itself lead to decreased motivation, especially when you're remote and isolated from colleagues. Reaching out to your peers and asking if anyone else is experiencing the same thing can help. Maybe the work has gotten monotonous, and it's not just you. Hearing a few words of solidarity and support go a long way.

Don't hesitate to take some time to reflect or even take a day off if you feel like you're in a rut. Remember, remote-first organizations typically value autonomy and high-focus work that delivers good output more than the hours you work or the speed at which you produce results. If you're not doing your best work, it's up to you (autonomously) to assess the situation and think through what's happening (prioritizing results over speed) so that you operate at your best consistently.

Using Existing Habits to Help Establish New Ones

No matter how long you've worked remotely, a key to establishing a healthy balance that preserves your personal life is to have habits. Habits are actions or activities that we do habitually, meaning we don't think much about them. You might have a habit of always putting on your seat belt when you get into a car or making coffee right after you wake up. They're things you rarely forget to do because you do them almost automatically.

In remote work, forming good habits around how and when you work helps you protect your personal life, because you do them without thought. Establishing new habits and getting them to stick is hard, though, as anyone who's ever changed their diet or quit smoking will tell you. It's easy to say you will do something new, but it's hard to do it consistently over time.

One trick to making new habits stick is to tie them to an existing habit. In remote work, this trick works really well for starting and ending the day, as well as taking planned breaks.

Starting Your Workday

In Chapter 3, you learned that a good strategy for starting your workday is to tie it to an existing habit, such as making coffee, writing in your journal, taking your vitamins, and so forth.

When people are new to remote work, they don't always think they need to find an existing habit to signal the start of the day. They think they can look at the clock and that will be enough. And sometimes it is. However, the clock can lose its power over time. For example, if you live somewhere with seasons, you might find that starting work at the same time every day is easy when the sun rises early and it's warm outside, but it becomes difficult when the weather starts to get cold and it's dark in the morning. Establishing a habit for how you start your day can thwart those kinds of problems in the future.

Ending Your Workday

You can use the same trick to end your workday by picking an existing habit and pinning the end of your working hours to it. For parents, childcare responsibilities might be the signal to end your workday. If you don't have a clear obligation or habit that happens around the same time that you want to end your workday, you might have to create one.

As mentioned in Chapter 3, an alternative solution is to make a commitment (walking your dog, promising to call a friend) or promise yourself a reward (doing a hobby or activity you enjoy). If there's an activity you previously enjoyed during your commute, such as listening to audiobooks or podcasts, you might try that.

ESSENTIAL

When you create a commitment or reward to end your day, you miss out on the benefit of having it pre-established, but you gain the ability to be strategic about it. Take going for a short walk as an example. It allows you to not only use an activity to mark the end of your day but also to get physical movement, take a mental break, and see some natural light. In other words, you get multiple benefits.

Commitments are useful for people who really struggle with shutting off from work. By making yourself accountable to other people, not just yourself, you can increase your chances of following through on the activity—and shutting down from work mode for the day!

Communicating with People Who Share Your Space

The people who share your space, including all household members regardless of whether they also work remotely, are not mind readers. They need to know what *you* need to work successfully and why. You have to clue them in to how their behaviors affect your ability to do your job.

With household members who also work remotely, the key to making the relationships work is overcommunicating and negotiating. Your fellow household members who don't work remotely might not have any idea how difficult it can be to balance your work and personal time, get past household distractions, and be good at your job despite some of the challenges of remote work. As a result, they may inadvertently take advantage of you and your remote work lifestyle.

Sharing Space with Other Remote Workers

What should you do if you're not the only person who works remotely in your home or place where you work? The best thing you can do is take those same overcommunication skills you've been developing at your job and apply them here.

Overcommunicate by talking about your plans and expectations for the day. Share your calendars with one another (as long as privacy concerns allow it) so you can be aware of times when one of you has a meeting. If you share a small space, give even more detail about when you have meetings, calls, and training sessions on the agenda so that the other person can plan their own quiet time, loud time, and time outside the workspace appropriately.

Also overcommunicate about whether you do or do not like being interrupted to chat, or what times of day you welcome it.

If children, other family members requiring care, or pets are in the mix, negotiate with the other adult household members who will handle care responsibilities throughout the day, especially when one of you needs to focus or participate in a meeting. If you have an important presentation or event on your calendar, tell the other person about it in advance. Remind them as the date gets closer, and ask if they can entertain the yappy dog or keep the crying baby out of earshot at that time.

Having another person coworking by your side can make remote work less isolating and more enjoyable too. It's nice to have someone who can hold you accountable to your promise of an afternoon walk outside, someone to eat lunch with, and someone who can help you out when you need it.

You're a Remote Worker, Not the House Manager

Not everyone who shares your personal space is with you while you work. When you are the sole person who works from home, other household members might start treating you like a house manager. Since you'll be home anyway, you can accept deliveries and let in a repair person. Since you have a flexible schedule, you can take the cat to the vet. Since you don't have to commute, you can make the kids' lunches before school.

ALERT

Undeniably, working remotely gives you flexibility, but it's unfair for other people in your home to assume you'll manage all the household responsibilities, including theirs, just because you can make yourself available when needed.

Have a conversation about these kinds of expectations as early as possible in your remote work career. Trying to talk about shared responsibilities after they've been overloaded on you (and perhaps after you're feeling bitter about them) is tough. Explain that you're perfectly happy to help out, but that it's unfair for someone else to always assume you're available. It impinges on your time and can affect your work when other people put pressure on you to handle every little obligation that arises.

If your partner or roommate or other adult household members work outside the home, they should occasionally have to take time away from their jobs to let in the Internet repair team or pick up a sick child from school. It shouldn't always be you.

Embracing the Perks of Remote Work and Working from Home

So much of making a remote work lifestyle work for you has to do with striking a balance between personal life and work life. A significant amount of energy and thought goes into establishing boundaries and rules to guide you toward a productive, healthy, and satisfying lifestyle.

Yet sometimes the best perks of working remotely have to do with the fact that your work time and personal time are not wholly separate, or that your workspace and living space are one and the same. You shouldn't always be expected to bend your schedule to take care of household needs, but you can when you need to. A yapping puppy might interrupt a meeting every so often, but the fact that you have a remote job allows you to be home for your pets, to bond with them, walk them, train them, and receive their love.

Pause to appreciate and embrace the perks of remote work from time to time so you don't take them for granted. Even though it can be challenging, there's so much to love about it.

CHAPTER 10

Ensuring Growth As a Remote Employee

Before remote work took off as a movement, the small percentage of people who did work remotely often struggled with growth and promotion. When remote work was still quite uncommon, there was a pervasive attitude that if someone wasn't physically present, they weren't well positioned to move into leadership roles. As these outdated attitudes recede and remote work culture corrects other wrong assumptions, there is a path to growth as a remote employee. It's largely driven by you, however, so you'll need a proactive attitude to get there.

How to Stay Relevant When You're Not Physically There

Out of sight, out of mind, right? One of the biggest fears in remote work is being passed up for opportunities and promotions because your boss, manager, and other people in the organization rarely see you face-to-face. The worry of slipping into the background is real.

Within the context of remote work, you can make yourself seen and heard in multiple ways.

Participate and Engage

When you participate and engage with others, rather than working in a silo, you make yourself seen and heard. Showing up to meetings allows you some virtual face time with your colleagues, bosses, and leadership team, which is why it's one of the easiest and most obvious ways to stay relevant. People literally see you and hear you.

What if there's an optional meeting that's consistently at a time that's inconvenient for you to attend? Or what if you're pretty introverted and know that meetings are not the best way for you to shine?

FACT

Research summarized in a 2012 *MIT Sloan Management Review* article found that remote employees (at organizations that also have in-person options), were prone to "lower performance evaluations, smaller raises, and fewer promotions," even when they worked as hard as their colleagues. A true remote-first approach should avoid this bias, but watch out for it in hybrid setups.

Meetings are hardly the only way to participate. Ask yourself how you best engage with others. Are you good at contributing to shared documents, asynchronous brainstorming, or probing new ideas with good questions? Where is your strong suit? Make yourself more visible by collaborating in all the ways that show your strengths. The hardest part is often not feeling self-conscious about chiming in and making yourself heard.

Make Use of Your In-Person Time

Remote workplaces very often have retreats, in-person team meetings, and other get-togethers every so often. When they occur, make the most of that in-person time to not only foster connections with your colleagues but also boost your presence to all those who oversee your career path.

How you go about doing so depends on the size of the organization and the purpose of the in-person gathering. Organization-wide retreats, for example, make for a good opportunity to get a few minutes of face time with people in the highest ranks of leadership. You don't have to schedule meetings with them or make it a formal affair. Wait for a time in the schedule set aside for socializing, such as meals or drinks, and simply find them and say hello.

Dedicate more time to your manager or boss, teammates, and anyone else with whom you collaborate regularly. In all likelihood, your team leader or manager will schedule some kind of social activity, even if it's just a shared meal, to help build camaraderie.

If you cannot attend events easily, whether for visa issues, care responsibilities, or any other reason, you might reach out to these same people and ask to have a virtual lunch or coffee with them in lieu of catching up in person.

ALERT

If you have to arrange virtual meetings because you can't attend an in-person event, do not schedule them in the week before, during, or after the live event. All the travel and coordination tend to drain people's energy. It's better to schedule time with people after they've sufficiently recovered from travel.

Case Study: Zapier's Twice-Annual Retreats

Zapier is an all-remote company with more than two hundred employees across thirty countries. Twice a year, it holds a weeklong retreat for the entire company at a destination usually in North America. Additionally, each team within the company (operations, support, product and design, marketing, and engineering) has its own smaller retreat once a year.

Erinique Owens is an event manager at Zapier who helps plan and run these get-togethers. "Retreats bring employees together to work on priority work as well as to bond and get to know each other," she says. They're the only times when employees, managers, and executives get face time. Having retreats "raises morale," Owens says, and they "add a sense of community and real-life connection."

The companywide retreats have several planned events, including a welcome dinner, scheduled time for in-person teamwork, and fun activities, such as beer tastings. The event team intentionally leaves a lot of free time on the schedule, too, so that people can connect, network, and get in more face-to-face interaction.

The Hybrid Dilemma

All this advice about staying relevant fits for people who operate in remote-first conditions. In hybrid organizations that haven't fully embraced the remote-first mindset, however, staying relevant and being heard can be more difficult.

The next chapter explores this dilemma in greater detail, but in short, when the organizational culture of a workplace undervalues remote work compared with in-person work, it puts you at a disadvantage when you're remote. If your contributions are undervalued when you're remote, it changes the dynamic of how other people see you, what kinds of opportunities you get, and whether you're passed over for mentoring, grooming, and promotions.

Developing a Proactive Attitude

If you're a freelancer, independent contractor, or other remote business of one, you already know that you must be proactive with your work and career if you want to succeed and progress. Being proactive means seeking new projects, clients, or work, and in particular, looking for opportunities that are in some way better or more lucrative than the ones you've done before. Rather than do the bare minimum of work and skate by, you must be a self-starter who looks for ways to improve and grow your business.

To do that, you might have to massage relationships, develop new skills (for example, learning to write proposals or marketing to promote your business), and in general, convince people that you offer something that's so high quality or unique that they should solicit your business. It's one of the hardest parts of working for yourself, but it's crucial.

Full-time remote employees benefit from adopting a similar attitude. The most valuable employees in any kind of job, remote or not, are usually the ones who take initiative (except in highly bureaucratic institutions where taking initiative can be seen as stepping out of line).

Self-starters are even more valuable in remote work due to the highly autonomous nature of how remote work occurs. Remote-first organizations rely on you to not just do the work in your job description but also to speak up when you have insights, new leads, or other ideas about how to improve or grow the business. Plus, most remote-first organizations like self-starters who use good judgment and "default to action." No one is going to coax you into making valuable suggestions—that's part of working autonomously. Your colleagues simply trust that you'll be proactive when you have something to share.

Make Your Boss's Job Easier

Managing people is hard, and not everyone is cut out for it. Managing people remotely is really hard.

ESSENTIAL

In an all-remote environment, you're not the only one struggling to figure out remote work. Everyone else in the organization, including the leadership team and your boss, are also learning how to work in a new way. As a result, they might not be great at giving advice or passing along opportunities that help you advance.

Part of your proactive attitude about remote work should be making your manager's job easier by managing yourself as much as possible. For example, ask for what you need explicitly rather than waiting for something to be offered. Suggest training you should get by finding a program and collecting the details about when it takes place, how much it costs, and so forth. State the promotion you want and begin a conversation about how you and your manager can map out a path together to get you there. When you do this proactive work, you make your boss's job much easier. Managers are much more likely to say yes to your ideas and suggestions when you do all the research and prep work.

Volunteer Before You're "Volun-Told"

When your team or organization are looking for volunteers, raise your hand from time to time.

In remote work, calls for volunteers are often done publicly, such as in an asynchronous collaboration app where everyone can see it. So unlike in a location-based environment, where you might quietly volunteer at your boss's verbal suggestion, in remote work everyone sees and knows when you step up.

You don't have to go overboard by joining every committee or pitching in for every special project. Rather, look for calls for volunteers for projects and work that you know matter deeply to the organization, even if it doesn't appeal to your personal or professional interests. When you volunteer to help with action items that are important to the organization, it helps you stand out as someone who's willing to pitch in when needed and try new things.

It's also helpful to volunteer for projects and work that might have low turnout. Sometimes people are asked to volunteer, and when not enough of them do, they're "volun-told." When you offer your services before one of your superiors has to forcibly persuade others into doing the work, that also helps you stand out in a positive way.

Meet New People

All the people in your professional sphere, including the so-called loose ties (business acquaintances, more or less), can potentially boost your career, improve your role, teach you something, or introduce you to new opportunities.

Meeting new people can be a challenge when you work remotely. Unless you're incredibly skilled at making friends online, it might not even cross your mind that you should be tending to and cultivating your network.

Large remote-first organizations sometimes have initiatives or programs to introduce employees to one another across departments or teams. The idea is to re-create so-called watercooler moments, where two people who don't know one another happen to strike up a conversation at the watercooler at in-person workplaces. If those programs aren't offered in your organization, look for other employee get-togethers where you might be able to meet folks beyond the bounds of your team.

FACT

Sometimes it's not who you know; it's who they know. In 1973, Mark S. Granovetter's "The Strength of Weak Ties" in the *American Journal of Sociology* showed that the majority of new job opportunities resulted from relationships that weren't very strong at all. The value, he argued, is not necessarily in the weak ties, but in how the tie links two people's associated groups. In other words, networking isn't just about you and one other person. It's about everyone else you both know.

Conferences and trade shows usually have networking time built into them. Even if you don't think you'll enjoy them, go to a few and exchange contact information with two or three people, just to give it a try.

Spread Your Contact Info

Another way to meet and network with people online is via social media, such as *Twitter*, *LinkedIn*, *Facebook*, *Instagram*, and *TikTok*, or professional online groups. If you want to encourage people to follow or connect with you on a site, include those details in your email signature, your online profiles, and your digital contact information, if you happen to share vCards with people.

FACT

A vCard is a file format that's meant to be a virtual business card. Typically, you enter data into your vCard using the contacts app on your phone or your email account. Then you can share it with others wirelessly. While they never quite took off as a replacement for business cards, vCards are convenient for getting all your contact details into someone else's address book quickly.

Conversely, when you receive emails from outside partners who include their social media handles in their signature lines, take a moment to look them up. They're providing that information because they want to network and connect. You can send the same message by adding your social media sites to your email signature too.

Tracking and Sharing Your Progress and Wins

To ensure growth in your career, occasionally you have to toot your own horn and let everyone know why you're so great at your job. To do that, you first have to know what your accomplishments are. What have you done in the past year that's noteworthy? How did you add value to the organization? What big wins did you have?

Typically, your manager will ask you for a list of your successes during your annual review, although sometimes you can slip in reminders of your greatness in a one-on-one or team meeting, as long as you do it appropriately and don't come off as having a gigantic ego.

That's all easier said than done, of course. A lot of jobs that can be done remotely don't have visible or easily measurable achievements, making it difficult to name them. And if your manager puts you on the spot and asks for a list of all the good work you've done, it can be really hard to think of them at that moment.

Prepare yourself with answers by keeping a running list of your accomplishments. That way, when the time is right to share them, you can reference your list and talk about your achievements eloquently.

So start writing down your accomplishments, milestones, and even compliments you receive.

Keep a Running List of Achievements

Start by making a folder somewhere. It can be on your computer's desktop or in email or in a note-taking app. Name the folder something like "Successes" or "Achievements." Every time you work on a big project, contribute to an important initiative, or volunteer at work, jot it down. What was the project? How did you contribute? When did it happen? It doesn't have to be much, just a few lines of detail to jog your memory.

When you're in the throes of work, major progress and achievements can blur into the hubbub of each day and week. If your organization uses OKRs, you can look to them for help pinpointing the achievements your team has made, which might help you put into words exactly how you contributed to them. With OKRs, someone (perhaps even you) has already defined what successes the team is striving for, and if you go back historically, you can pluck out the examples that are relevant.

Another source you can mine for achievements is regular stand-up meetings with your team or one-on-ones with your manager. If someone gives a nod to your work, write it down. If your manager shares notes with you after your one-on-ones, copy any words of congratulations on a job well done into your own notes.

ESSENTIAL

The real reason you should mine OKRs and meeting notes for your achievements is because someone has already done the work for you. Gathering a list of your accomplishments is work about work, not core work, which you should try to minimize. If someone has already done the work for you, use it!

Over time, the highlights will become apparent from your list, and that's your starting point for naming your successes and wins.

Save Compliments

Save or write down compliments and positive feedback that people give you too. You can use them as a source of inspiration whenever you need examples of how you add value to the organization.

Don't forget to record verbal compliments and feedback. You can jot them down in the same place where you store other notes about your successes.

Recirculate Positive Feedback

When people give you positive feedback, don't keep it to yourself. Share it up the chain. If clients, partners, team members in other departments, or customers go out of their way to express gratitude for your work, that's all valuable evidence that you're good at your job.

When you have a relationship with a person who's given you positive feedback, thank them and, if it's appropriate, ask if they would be so kind as to pass it along to your manager or leadership team. If it's not appropriate, make a record of it for yourself and consider sharing it with your manager when a good time presents itself.

As mentioned, there's a delicate balance between sharing positive feedback and seeming like a person with an inflated ego who's promoting themself too hard. Make it part of normal conversation: "Can I share with you some positive feedback I got? It made me feel good to hear it." That's enough to make the intention of the conversation clear.

Complimenting Others Helps You Be Seen and Heard

When you get stuck and don't know how to participate in ways that make you seen and heard, there's one reliable fallback: Share positive feedback. The people receiving this feedback will appreciate hearing it, and it's an easy way to speak up without making it about you. It's also just a kind and considerate way to be a good coworker. Who did great work recently that you noticed but other people didn't? What's something helpful or uplifting about the way your team collaborates? What do you like about the way people communicate with you?

You don't have to kiss up or be too saccharine about positive feedback. Look for it in the everyday motions of work. If you have no major complaints about your job, something is probably going right. Rather than let good work go unnoticed, try to identify it and tell people about it.

You can even give positive feedback for things that people don't do. Here's an example: "Can I share some positive feedback? I really appreciate that you didn't participate in the team chat channel last week while you were on vacation. When you and other colleagues disconnect from work to enjoy your time off, it helps me feel secure in doing it too."

Remember to phrase your feedback in a constructive way—"When you do this, the outcome is that"—and don't dangle it. Tell the person you have feedback and deliver the feedback clearly in one go.

Perhaps this suggestion may sound too strategic, but try setting a recurring reminder on your to-do list or in your calendar to look for and give positive feedback once a month or every other week. It's so easy to forget to do it, yet it becomes so easy when you practice it like any other skill.

Tips for Working with Managers and Bosses

In no small part, your bosses and managers play a role in your professional trajectory. They are largely responsible for whether you get the recognition you deserve at work.

How you interact and work with your managers and bosses in a remote environment might be a little different and more explicit than what you may have experienced in location-based work.

Tell Your Manager How You're Best Managed

Managers have different managing styles. Some remote managers are very hands-on. They check in on you often. They're quick to ask how things are going and if you need anything. These types of managers actively prevent problems, or try to anyway. The motivation to manage in this style usually comes from a good place. Hands-on managers can be caring and highly invested in your success. For some employees, however, this style can come off as micromanaging, highly interruptive, and downright bothersome.

On the other end of the management style spectrum are hands-off managers. This style of manager believes that no news is good news. If they don't hear anything from you, they assume everything is going swimmingly. They trust that if you need something or have a question, you'll speak up. Hands-off managers allow you to make decisions and work independently. Some employees, however, feel abandoned and neglected by this management style.

In remote work, you can and should have an ongoing conversation with your manager about what type of management style works best for you. Do you thrive when left alone to concentrate and get work done, or do you feel more supported and encouraged when someone checks in with you frequently? Maybe you don't know yet! Make it an ongoing conversation so that it can change with time or with different work assignments. If you're taking on new assignments at work, perhaps you want more intervention when you're learning how to do them.

ALERT

If your manager's style just happens to fit your working style perfectly and you don't need adjustments, give that feedback too! Pinpoint why it works for you. That affirmation will help your manager continue working with you in the right ways.

Share What's Going Well

In any type of work, remote or not, employees should let their boss or manager know when something's wrong. In remote work, it's just as important to do the opposite and tell them what is working.

Without much face-to-face interaction or ability to observe people collaborating in real time, managers don't always have a good sense of the team dynamic. Because most people don't speak up when everything's running smoothly, managers need reassurance. If you don't tell them that things are going well, how will they know?

When you reassure your managers that the team dynamic is solid and that your work is going well, it can alleviate pressure and make their jobs easier. When their job is easier, they have more time and energy to work with you on important issues, like laying out a path for your career growth.

Asking for What You Need and the Growth You Want

In any job, you might wonder when you will get promoted or how your career will progress and how long it will take for each step to happen. In remote work, where you interact much less with your colleagues and managers compared with in-person work, it can feel like you are completely in the dark about your path to growth, unless you take action.

Everything about creating a path for personal growth ties back to the themes of overcommunication, making your boss's job easier, and taking initiative. Ultimately, you are responsible for (1) deciding what you want from your job and career, (2) coming up with a rough plan for it, and (3) communicating it clearly to your managers and bosses.

Keep Your Options Open

Not everyone knows from the get-go what they want. When working for an interesting organization, you might learn about new job roles and responsibilities that you didn't even know existed. Maybe you start out working as a product manager but through close contact with the research and development team, you decide over time that you'd rather work in that area. It's perfectly acceptable to adjust your plan for growth on the fly.

Be Clear and Precise When You Know What You Want

With in-person work, coworkers and bosses can get ideas about your strengths and where they'd like to see you advance without always asking you if it's what you want. They see you throughout the week and overhear conversations that point to what you do well, and the next thing you know, someone is steering you into a position that you don't want, because they assumed you'd be good at it. Being capable at a job and wanting it are two different things.

In remote work, however, your strengths and weaknesses are not always as apparent, which can actually give you more agency. If your superiors make fewer assumptions about what you can do, what you're interested in, and so forth, they could be in a better position to hear it from you directly.

If you're among the lucky few who know what they want, being in a remote-first organization is a great place to express it. You should still be strategic in how much you share about your grand dreams—if, for example, it means eventually outgrowing your current organization and moving to one that's bigger or more prestigious, or starting your own. Focus on the path you want within your current organization and share that. Be clear and specific so that people can help you achieve your goal.

Find the Right Coach

A good manager should coach you through your career plan, although as mentioned, not every manager is a good one. If your manager or boss isn't helpful in giving you advice and shaping your path forward, find someone who can.

Ask to be paired with a mentor in your organization or look for someone outside the organization who might mentor you formally or informally. A business coach might also help. If you're employed full-time, the cost of a business coach might even be covered or reimbursable.

Using One-on-Ones to Voice Your Plan for Growth or Promotion

Creating (getting down to specific details) and making known your plan for growth or promotion should happen mostly in your one-on-one meetings with your manager.

As you'll recall, the one-on-one is a regularly scheduled meeting, typically once a week, when you and your manager discuss anything you need between just the two of you. In remote work, these meetings are the primary moments when you and your manager have synchronous time together.

You'll also remember that you should be driving the one-on-one meetings as much as possible. Don't leave the full agenda up to your manager. A good manager will explain this, but one that lacks training might not know. Take initiative to write an agenda beforehand and drive the meeting.

How to Bring Up Your Career

When you first started your job or perhaps even during the job interview, you might have discussed your intended career plans with the hiring committee and your manager. A great way to open the conversation with your manager is to revisit what you said then.

What questions did people ask you during the interview about your career plans? Or what information did you offer? Are your plans still the same now?

As you bring up this point, ask your manager for their thoughts and reactions. Does this career path sound achievable? What should you do to get there? By encouraging your manager's input, you give them an active role in the process, which ultimately helps you because your manager is the person who can assist you best.

Be ready to revisit your plan every few weeks or months to check whether you've made progress, develop the plans with new details, and adjust your goals if they've changed.

When the kind of career growth that you want involves moving into another department, it's to your benefit to bring up the idea slowly over time, rather than spring it on your boss out of the blue. You can express interest in something new without making it sound like you're ready to abandon your current role. A good way to start is to say, "I'd like to learn more about how that department works," or "I'm interested in how that department connects with what we do in ours." Your boss or manager should encourage you to explore that area of interest, but if they don't, you can strike out on your own to set up an informational interview with someone from that other department. An informational interview is essentially a meet-and-greet where someone tells you about the work they do and you get to ask questions. Afterward, if you're still interested, you'll have another person to ask for advice about what skills you need or how to position yourself to possibly make the switch. Take your time with it so you don't catch anyone by surprise.

Ask for Specific Tasks and Responsibilities

As you and your manager develop this plan for your growth, ask for specific tasks and responsibilities that will put you in the right direction. For example, if you want to learn some of your boss's responsibilities to eventually advance in that direction, ask if there's anything you can cover for them the next time they take leave, and be clear that the reason is for you to develop new skills. If you want to manage people, ask about the best way to get started. You might be able to oversee an intern or a volunteer, or maybe mentor a new employee or manage a few pieces of their work.

Be as specific as possible in the exact tasks and responsibilities that you need to reach the next milestone in your advancement. Again, it helps to lay the groundwork in advance during your one-on-ones so that by the time you're asking for the opportunity to learn a skill or take on new responsibility, you can remind your boss that doing so is in line with the career goals you've already discussed.

Be Patient

Getting promoted and moving up in your career takes time, usually years. If you don't make significant movement within the first year on a job, relax. It's not necessarily the case that people have forgotten about you in your isolated remote role. More likely, it just hasn't happened yet.

Focus on the very specific new tasks, responsibilities, and skills you and your manager have identified that you need to develop to make progress. If after a year you haven't gotten an opportunity to do or learn any of them, speak up. That shouldn't be the case if you've been able to check in on and discuss your career plan every few weeks in your one-on-one meetings. If it is, however, ask your manager why and how you can work together to change that going forward.

Seizing Opportunities for Continued Learning

Remote-first organizations tend to be small or medium-sized, a few hundred employees at most. (Historically, there have been notable exceptions, such as IBM, but they're rare.) Generally speaking, small and medium-sized organizations lack the structure for career advancement that large organizations sometimes offer. At a large organization, for example, you might be on the "management track" with a clear two-year program for training and development to advance you into a management position. That's almost never the case at smaller organizations, and as such it's rare among remote-first businesses.

While your manager may help you plot a path for your career progression within the organization, it's up to you to seek out additional ways to learn and develop skills that you might not be able to learn on the job or from your immediate colleagues. When you teach yourself new things beyond the walls of the organization, you also help the organization grow, and that's a valuable asset that can help you earn distinction.

Online Learning

Online learning programs have never been as high in quality or as varied as they are now. You can learn soft skills, such as how to communicate effectively in a globalized workforce, and hard skills, such as programming languages.

QUESTION

How do I know if an online learning course is any good?
Read the course description or syllabus and look for ratings from other learners who took the course. If there are no user ratings, look for reputable, professional reviews of the host site. Lastly, take advantage of any free versions of the course that are available or a free trial period so you can try the first lesson.

When you have an idea of how you want your career to progress, seek out classes that will teach you what you need to know to move forward. Try to be specific and look for instruction that's at the right level for you. For example, if you want to learn how to code but you have zero experience, find a series of courses that are for true beginners. One class isn't going to teach you everything, so look for a longer program. If you want to advance in a role where you already have some experience, however, look for classes that offer inspiration and advice in addition to straightforward training. When you already know a lot of tips and tricks for getting your job done, the route to advancement is often learning to think differently and more strategically about your work and its role in the organization.

A wealth of online learning is free, though some programs require tuition fees or paid subscriptions. Always ask whether your organization will cover these fees before enrolling. When you ask, give a clear and concise summary of the course and how it will benefit not only you but also your team and the organization.

Conferences and Workshops

Conferences, workshops, and other special events offer you more ways to learn new skills and knowledge to do your job better and eventually advance. (They're good for networking too.) More and more, these events are being offered online, making them more accessible; and you or your employer don't have to pay for related travel expenses to attend.

Finding conferences and workshops can be a bit of a crapshoot. Larger conferences usually happen on an annual schedule, but smaller workshops can pop up at any time.

You can always ask your colleagues, especially those who are senior to you, if they know of any good ones you might attend. Additionally, following people on social media who are in your field can bring events to your attention. When a major event happens, you'll see people in your field using hashtags for it. Smaller workshops may even be run by the people you follow, and they'll promote them online.

CHAPTER 11

Mastering the Hybrid Model

The hybrid model blends in-person and remote work, and it's a dicey proposition. The problem is that many organizations adopt it without first changing anything about how they do business. Like any other remote-work arrangement, the hybrid model needs to operate under a remote-first mindset to succeed. Otherwise, the organization is setting up all its remote work time to be less effective. If you're going to go hybrid, you have to first embrace a remote-first attitude.

What Is a Hybrid-Remote Work Model?

In a hybrid-remote work model, an organization supports a blend of in-person work and remote work. Exactly how it looks can vary tremendously.

Roots of the Hybrid Idea

The idea of hybrid-remote work only became popular during the 2020 COVID-19 pandemic, when schools were forced to adopt a hybrid model for teaching. When it became abundantly clear that an all-remote education system wouldn't work for all ages, all students, all subjects, or all parents, many schools latched on to the idea that students could be split into two cohorts, with each cohort attending school in person two days per week (different days for different cohorts) and learning remotely the other three days a week.

Prior to 2020, almost no one in the business world talked about hybrid workplaces. The idea picked up steam, however, after employees were forced to work remotely due to the pandemic, proved they could do it, and declared that they wanted to continue doing it. Suddenly, employers realized that taking away the option to work remotely would be an uphill battle (like trying to put a genie back in the bottle).

A/B Teams

There were some types of organizations using the hybrid approach to work during the coronavirus pandemic that weren't influenced by schools, but they are a special case. Most of them are businesses or governmental organizations who have some work that can be done remotely and other work that requires being at a secure site. In these types of workplaces, a hybrid approach called the A/B schedule or AA/BB schedule took off.

As with schools, it was used primarily to reduce the potential spread of disease to an entire workforce by creating two teams. Team A works together on-site two days per week, and Team B does the same but on two different days. So Team A might go to the job site Monday and Tuesday, while Team B goes on Thursday and Friday. The remaining day, Wednesday, is reserved for cleaning and maintenance. If someone on Team A becomes infected, everyone on Team A quarantines and gets tested as necessary, while Team B continues working without interruption.

While this system is good for reducing the spread of diseases, the A/B schedule doesn't really serve other purposes, so it's not likely to become the permanent schedule for most employers.

Flexwork

Before 2020, there was another popular approach to remote work: flexwork, or flex time. As it stands now, "flexwork" and "hybrid" aren't quite interchangeable terms, but they could become so over time.

Flexwork starts from the premise that work is primarily done in-person at a shared fixed location; however, some employees may choose to work remotely either when they need to or on a fixed schedule, such as every Friday. With flexwork, employees are never mandated to work remotely. It's always an opt-in choice, and it typically requires approval. Some employees like that it gives them a little flexibility for an otherwise in-person job.

Flexwork benefits employers in at least two ways, and it's important to know what they are so you know what you are getting into and can see the dynamic between you and the employer for what it is. One benefit for employers is that employees (that's you) can work more. You don't have to take a full day off work for a case of the sniffles, to wait for a repair person, or to keep an eye on a sick child. Second, flexwork is usually at the employer's or manager's discretion, which means they can deny it or take it away if it's not working in their favor.

One way employers don't benefit, however, is saving on office space and furniture. Flexwork is built on an in-person premise, so the employer must offer a workspace that can hold all its employees and all the equipment and furniture they need. That's not necessarily the case with other types of hybrid approaches, where the employer can mandate that employees work remotely a certain percentage of the time, thereby allowing them to condense physical office space and reduce costs. In this sense, it's possible to have an organization of three hundred people and yet have physical space for only one hundred at a time.

Other Hybrid-Like Options

There are other ways to blend in-person and remote work within one organization. For example, it's not unheard of for the majority of employees of an organization to work in person while a select few people work remotely on a permanent basis. Another configuration could be to have one primary work site, such as a headquarters, plus some satellite locations, and a blend of in-person work and remote work across them all.

Is Hybrid Work Right for You?

If you have a choice to work for an organization with a hybrid model, or your current employer starts offering hybrid options, how do you know you should take part in it?

A good place to start is to evaluate whether it's truly a choice or is mandated. Is the arrangement flexible enough that you could try it out and make changes if it's not working? Will you be treated the same regardless of whether you're at the work site versus remote?

FACT

According to a January 2021 survey about work published by Microsoft, 73 percent of full-time and self-employed workers want flexible remote work options, and 67 percent said that after the COVID-19 pandemic ends, they want more in-person work or collaboration opportunities.

There are a lot of questions to ask and pros and cons to weigh. Already you can see that hybrid work often has uncertainty baked into it. Answers to three questions will resolve much of that uncertainty for you:

- Has the organization planned and prepared to be hybrid?
- Are employees allowed to choose how they participate, or is it mandated?
- Will it be equitable?

Did the Organization Plan to Be Hybrid?

Taking an existing in-person business and simply asking people to sometimes work remotely doesn't create a foundation on which you can succeed.

If an employer has clear policies and a remote-first attitude toward how it operates, then you're in fairly good hands to start. You want to know that there's been some level of intentional planning and decision-making from the top to actively support a hybrid environment.

The reverse conditions really set you up for failure. If the organization decides to wing it and not create any policies or do any planning for how it will operate differently in a hybrid environment, you'll be left to work in highly unstable and undefined conditions.

How Much Agency Will You Have?

A huge predictor in whether people are successful working remotely is whether they choose to do so. When remote work is mandated and you have no say in when or how often you're remote versus at the work site, you have no agency. When you have little to no agency, you're prohibited from working in the ways that you know are best for you and your success. Plus, generally speaking, workers with less agency are less satisfied with their jobs.

The best you can hope for in a hybrid environment is the option to work remotely sometimes (to opt in) and the ability to negotiate when you do it. You don't necessarily need complete control over your schedule to be happy working in a hybrid situation, but you should have some input to make sure the results work for you.

Will It Be Equitable?

Another question you may want to ask yourself before deciding to jump into a hybrid organization—or as you learn to navigate hybrid options if you're already in one—is whether people are treated equitably when they are remote versus in-person.

If an organization hasn't made changes to its culture and structure to support remote work, then in-person employees may be at a significant advantage. For example, if the leadership team works mostly in person rather than remotely, then all the people who work on-site the most get more face time with them. Those additional interactions can cause the leaders to think of the in-person employees first for interesting projects and other opportunities that result in promotions and advancement. Anyone who needs to work remotely most of the time ends up disadvantaged in this way.

QUESTION

What should I do if I'm disadvantaged because I work remotely the majority of the time?
Speak up. If you believe you're missing out on opportunities, ask for more opportunities. If the problem persists, you can raise the concern that you worry you're missing out by being remote. Try to keep an attitude of looking for a resolution rather than complaining.

With an intentional remote-first approach, however, everyone should be treated more or less equally, even in a hybrid workplace. Leaders in the organization are more likely to be aware of potential biases toward employees who are in person than they are of others, and they can talk openly about how to mitigate them. There will always be differences in how people at work interact and get their jobs done when they are in person versus remote, but the majority of work in a hybrid office should get done the same way regardless of who is remote and who is sitting at a desk in an office. It should default to getting done in the remote way first.

Reaping the Rewards of a Hybrid Work Lifestyle

The hybrid work lifestyle is most suited to those who enjoy being at a work site with other people (maybe even prefer it to being remote) but like having the option to work remotely sometimes.

It's a great fit if you don't mind commuting, appreciate getting out of the home to be somewhere else for a few hours, and like having the boundaries of a workplace, but don't necessarily want to partake in them every day. As previously mentioned, it's ideal to have some agency in choosing when and how often you are remote, but even if someone else makes the schedule for you, it still could be a good fit.

The Benefits of Going to Work

In a hybrid model, you can reap the rewards of going to a workplace while also taking advantage of the unique benefits that remote work provides.

Going to work has its benefits. You get out of the house at a reliable time, ramp up for work on the commute in, and wind down on the commute home. You might even be friends with some of your coworkers, in which case it's nice to see them regularly.

A workplace also isn't home. It's another place to be. If full-time remote work gives you cabin fever because you find it psychologically difficult to find a reason to leave, then the routine of going to work is probably pleasant. Going to work also gives you physical separation between your personal life and your work life.

ESSENTIAL

Not everyone experiences the perceived benefits of going to a workplace as beneficial. If you find that going to a job site is overrated, you're probably better suited to an all-remote role or a hybrid role that lets you work remotely the majority of the time and show up in person seldomly.

Even for hybrid workers, the benefits of going to work aren't always all they're cracked up to be. Sometimes you want to sleep in or the weather is lousy and commuting is an awful experience. Every now and again, it makes sense to take care of personal responsibilities from home while continuing to work. The hybrid model can give you that level of flexibility, depending on the arrangement and whether you choose your schedule or someone else decides it for you.

Agency—having some say over your schedule and being able to negotiate it in your favor—is a big deal. The more agency you have, the more you can reap the rewards of both in-person and remote work.

Make the Most of Your In-Person Time

As you get savvy about working in a hybrid setup, you'll learn to make the most of your in-person time by asking what you can do only in person and what you do best there.

Being at a shared work location gives you synchronous time with others. How you make the most of your time there overlaps significantly with how you make the most of your time in a virtual, synchronous meeting. To recap those ideas, synchronous time with others is best for:

- Brainstorming and discussing ideas quickly
- Fostering connections among people and getting to know one another
- Having conversations where questions, clarification, and additional information are expected
- Having conversations where tone of voice, facial expressions, and body language add significant meaning
- Making decisions quickly

Make the Most of Your Remote Time

Just as you'll want to take advantage of what you can do when you're on-site at a job, you'll also want to make the most of your remote time.

For example, in most circumstances, you can better control external interruptions and distractions when you're remote. That in turn gives you longer and more frequent stretches of uninterrupted time to do core work that requires high focus. You can take care of personal responsibilities, such as light household chores and being available to receive deliveries or let service people into your home while also working. Because you can choose where you work when you're remote, you can work remotely during the same times when you travel, whether that travel is for fun or an obligation. For example, imagine someone in your family recently gave birth and you want to go meet the new baby. You might only be welcomed around the new baby an hour or two at a time. In that case, it might make sense to work remotely during your visit rather than take time off. Or say you need to work because of a deadline, but the rest of your family wants to take a long weekend to visit their grandparents. If you have flexibility in when you work remotely, you can take the trip as planned and spend time with everyone while stepping away for a few hours to meet your deadline. As long as you can plan when you get to work remotely, you can make the most of your time.

Evaluating the Challenges of Hybrid Employment

By far the greatest challenge to working a hybrid schedule has to do with how well the organization designed its culture, practices, and policies to support it. But of course, you have little to no control over that.

There are more personal challenges, however, that you may face even if your employer does everything right to support you and your colleagues working in a hybrid setup.

The Schedule

The schedule is one of the most important parts of hybrid work to get right, and it's an incredibly tough skill to master. Your individual schedule is just one piece of the puzzle. Will you work remotely two days a week, once a month, on occasion as needed, or for the majority of the time and come into the workplace only once or twice a month? If your schedule isn't firm, how will your managers and coworkers know when you're available in person or what hours you're working remotely?

Now remember that all your coworkers have to determine their schedules, too, which affects how and when you collaborate with them, as well as how well you get to know them.

Loss of Personalized Space at Work

Another issue related to scheduling is whether you will have a permanent and personalized workstation at your workplace. Employers don't want to pay for physical space, furniture, and other equipment for employees who come to the workplace only once or twice a month on top of paying for the equipment they need when they work remotely. Instead, the workplace might be a flexible open space, plus a couple of conference rooms, where you make a spot for yourself every time you show up. Or there could be workstations that any employee can use. In other words, you might sit there for a day, but the desk, chair, and equipment aren't solely used by you (this is sometimes called "hot-desking"—described in more detail later in this chapter). Anyone can use the workstation as long as it isn't occupied.

As a result, you don't have a space of your own the way you might if you worked full-time in person. That can make the workplace feel less personalized and less comfortable, affecting your attitude when you're there.

Getting to Know Your Coworkers

Yet another issue that relates back to scheduling is how you get to know and develop trust with your coworkers. In a full-time remote situation, getting to know people takes time and may feel strange at first, but everyone has the same advantages and disadvantages, more or less. With a hybrid workplace, however, whom you see in person and spend time with may be at the whim of the schedule.

FACT

Developing relationships with coworkers may get easier the longer you work remotely. According to a Pew Research Center report, 65 percent of people who were new to remote work in 2020 felt less connected to their coworkers, while only 27 percent of experienced remote workers felt the same.

With the luck of the draw, you might be face-to-face with a few colleagues regularly and get to know them well. As you get to know people better, it can be easier to ask them questions or talk informally about work in ways that lead to information sharing or new ideas. (Who hasn't learned something valuable through dumb luck based on who else was in the room when you complained or asked a question?)

The relationships you have with colleagues you've never met in person might not be the same. And whether you meet them in person at all could come down to the schedule. This is yet another reason it's so important for organizations to plan for a hybrid model and be intentional about how they design it.

Limits to Developing Routines

With a hybrid setup, it can take longer and be harder to establish good working routines and habits. Working remotely only a few days a month doesn't give you enough practice at it to figure out your rhythm, learn how you work best, observe changes in your environment that you might need to work around (such as learning when the neighbor mows the lawn), and so forth. The sheer fact of not doing it every day makes it challenging.

The same thing can happen with your in-person routine. Being at the workplace only occasionally can make it feel disruptive. Are your coworkers the same each day you show up, or do they have different schedules? Do your expectations for what it's like to work at work constantly shift? With less certainty and ever-changing conditions, you might never really settle into the job or the best way for you to do it.

Boundaries? What Boundaries?

Going to work every day in person at a job site creates boundaries between personal life and work life, or that's the assumption at least. How does that assumption change if you go to work on Wednesday and then come home and stay home through all of Thursday and Friday to work remotely? Can you mentally leave your work behind in the workplace if you're always picking it back up again later from your kitchen table?

How good are workplace boundaries if they aren't consistent? At least with full-time remote work, you can be consistent in your routine and develop habits that help you create other kinds of boundaries, such as emotional and time-based boundaries, that let you keep work separate from your personal time. As mentioned, a hybrid work schedule makes it much harder to develop a routine because you're doing the activities that you want to turn into habits less frequently, so they don't stick as easily.

Setting Up a Hybrid Workplace

How you set up spaces to work when you're working in a hybrid approach depends a little bit on how much time you will spend in each of your work locations. Generally speaking, it makes sense to create an enjoyable and customized workspace for your remote time, no matter how frequently or infrequently you're there. When it comes to your setup for working in person, however, you may have less control over what you get, if you get anything at all.

Your Remote Workspace

Depending on how often you work remotely, you might not feel motivated to invest much thought, time, energy, and money into creating a dedicated workspace. Consider doing it anyway. The time you spend working remotely should be a positive experience. If you're uncomfortable or you dislike your space, you won't be able to make the most of being remote.

Make yourself a dedicated space and personalize it to be comfortable for you. Not necessarily right away, but over time, see how you feel about your chair, desk, lighting, and other key features that make a workstation pleasant or dreadful.

If your employer embraces a remote-first approach, which is the ideal, then you'll likely use your remote workspace (for example, your home) for work that requires high focus and uninterrupted stretches of time, and your in-person time for things you can only do at the work site, such as having in-person meetings and getting face time with your colleagues and superiors. So when crafting your remote workspace, think about what you need to be comfortable for the type of work you'll be doing there. In many cases, it will be high-focus work, but depending on your job, it could be making sales calls or giving training workshops to other remote employees. Make sure your remote workstation is built to support the tasks you plan to do there.

There are exceptions, of course. If you have personal circumstances, such as intense care responsibilities at home, that make the work site your best place to focus, then you might save your toughest tasks for when you're on-site. Alternatively, you might invest in a membership to a coworking space so that you have a better remote work spot than your home.

Hot-Desking in an Office

One major difference between a hybrid role and full-time location-based work is that when you are at the workplace in a hybrid role, you might not have your own desk, office, or even computer.

FACT

Hot-desking is an in-person system for working in which employees can work from any available desk on an ad hoc basis. These desks may have computer workstations, where each employee can access their own virtual space with a unique login. Or the desks can be empty and employees bring their laptops and other equipment.

Organizations that use a hybrid model may be looking to save money on office space and furniture. For that reason, they aren't going to give each employee their own physical space. It wouldn't make sense financially speaking. That's why they use hot-desking.

ALERT

If your organization adopted a hybrid model suddenly (such as after the 2020 COVID-19 pandemic), it might take years before it cuts office space because offices often have yearslong leases. It might not even have the option to reduce those costs for another ten years. If you're not hot-desking yet, it doesn't mean you won't be later.

While hot-desking can be efficient for the organization, it can also be less comfortable and less enjoyable for workers. When you don't have your own personal space at work, there are no desk drawers or display areas for photos, plants, snacks, or a sweater. If you're lucky, you might get a locker or other space where you can keep some comfort items so that you don't have to constantly bring them with you.

When hot-desking, you also don't necessarily have a dedicated chair, monitor, or other equipment, which means you have to readjust all the settings to fit you ergonomically every time you go to work in person.

CHAPTER 12

Becoming a Digital Nomad

If you can work from anywhere, why not travel the world while you do it? That's the sentiment at the heart of the digital nomad lifestyle. Theoretically, as long as you have an Internet connection and the equipment you need to work, you can bop from place to place, exploring all those far-flung destinations of your bucket list dreams. Before you romanticize the idea too much, you should know that being a digital nomad comes with plenty of challenges, and it's not a lifestyle that's available to everyone.

Who and What Are Digital Nomads?

Digital nomads, also sometimes described as location-independent, are people who work remotely and do not live in one fixed location for an extended period of time because they prioritize traveling. There are no rules about how long or short of a time they stay in any one place. Many move from city to city or country to country until they discover somewhere that they enjoy, and then they might stay a few weeks, months, or even a year or two. A tiny portion of digital nomads live in recreational vehicles or on boats and are constantly on the move.

FACT

According to a 2018 report from MBO Partners, about 69 percent of digital nomads identify as male, and 54 percent are older than thirty-eight. More than half (54 percent) put in full-time hours, and most are independent workers rather than employees. Only about 16 percent of digital nomads say they earn $75,000 or more.

The majority of digital nomads are self-employed types, such as freelancers and contractors (according to data from MBO Partners), but they can be employed full-time in remote positions. It's just less common.

That said, when a full-time employee tries to live and work from a new country, their employer must be involved in hashing out the legal issues, such as getting the required visa to work in each country. As a result, remote-first employers might have policies that protect them from getting into sticky legal territory, and those policies can limit the employee's ability to commit to a digital nomad lifestyle. That's just one reason being a digital nomad is more popular among self-employed people. They're solely responsible for their legal matters.

How to Make a Location-Independent Life Work

Figuring out how to make a location-independent life possible is more than just a numbers game. Calculating how much money you need to earn to be able to live in a certain part of the world is merely one step.

There are the logistics of organizing your life and your belongings. You have to determine where you can go, how long you're allowed to stay, and clear all the legal hurdles for going there. If you have children or other family members traveling with you, you'll have to have many conversations about their lives and needs. How will you handle schooling? What do your family members want out of life for their own fulfillment? How important is it to be able to visit extended family while traveling, and how frequently will you do it?

If you're traveling solo, you'll also have to think about your personal life and what you need to allow it to develop and grow. How will you make friends? Will you study the local language if you don't speak it? What about your career? Sure, you might be able to earn money from anywhere in the world, but will you have what you need to advance your career and keep it from stagnating?

You can address some of these questions as you live a digital nomad life, learning and figuring it out as you go, though some you should think about and discuss with others deeply before committing to making the leap.

How Long Can the Lifestyle Last?

Starting and maintaining a location-independent life requires you to balance the ability to plan with the ability to be open to change depending on what happens. Some digital nomads may commit to the lifestyle for a set period of time, such as one year or five years. Many others don't know how, when, or why their digital nomad lifestyle will end.

ESSENTIAL

Anecdotally, digital nomads seem to transition out of the lifestyle within five years of starting, though some stick with it longer. It's also possible to be location-independent for a while, then settle down, and eventually start up again. The digital nomad mentality is all about freedom and personal empowerment, so you choose the terms.

While there isn't necessarily a reason to plan in advance for a specific end date, it may help to always keep in the back of your mind that there may be one someday. Believing "once a digital nomad, always a digital nomad" might cut you off from thinking about all the possible future achievements you might want out of your professional or personal life. Accepting that it will probably come to a conclusion one day may help you keep a healthy perspective throughout the journey.

Passport Privilege

Narratives around the digital nomad lifestyle like to say that travel is within reach for anyone! They say it doesn't have to be outlandishly expensive. You can let go of your worldly possessions, cash them in for a plane ticket, and take off to live and work in some new, exciting place, especially if you go where the cost of living is low.

What's missing from that picture, however, is the power of the passport. Passport holders of a few wealthy nations have a much easier time accessing international travel than many other people around the world. The ease of getting a visa varies dramatically based on the country listed on the front of your passport.

So as much as the digital nomad life is hyped as being available to anyone who wants to do it, that's really not the case at all.

Accessibility

Another factor that affects whether people can participate in a digital nomad life is accessibility. People with wheelchairs, crutches, and other mobility aids already know that worldwide, destinations with a low cost of living often lack accessibility infrastructure.

The availability and accessibility of medical care and medications are another factor, even for relatively healthy people. For example, if you need a regular supply of diabetes medication, figuring out in advance where in the world you can live and still get your medications reliably, not to mention whether you'll need to find a local doctor to write the prescription—well, these are not trivial matters that you can just deal with on the fly. They can change the possibilities of where you can go and how long you can stay.

> **ESSENTIAL**
>
> Being a digital nomad isn't the only way to explore the world while working remotely. Other opportunities, such as applying for grants, fellowships, and international programs, come with a little more structure (and funding) that may make it easier for people with different needs to work remotely from a new place.

In-Country Digital Nomads

Digital nomads aren't necessarily international travelers. In the US and other large countries or regions such as the European Union, you could easily spend years exploring without ever boarding a plane or needing your passport. In the case of the US, you also have a few territories, including Puerto Rico and the US Virgin Islands, within reach.

Even as a US resident, however, you still may face limitations related to medical care access in different states, which will be covered further later in this chapter.

Navigating Working Hours and Time Zones

Digital nomads have to be flexible like never before in working with clients and their time zones. As with any remote work, if you collaborate with or work for people who understand the concept of remote-first, then you should be able to get your work done in whatever time frame you choose. Still, when it comes to connecting with people, such as answering client messages and taking calls, you have to be flexible and willing to work at possibly inconvenient times. It doesn't hurt to bring a cheery attitude when you do it.

Remember that you're the party who chooses to never stay in one place for very long and hop across time zones willy-nilly. That's why it's on you to accommodate other people's schedules. Sure, you can always try to find a time to meet with a client or colleague that works for both of you, but when someone has to bend over backward to make it work, it's going to be you.

If you're a media personality or influencer, the same goes for any podcasts, television or radio spots, or other promotional appearances that you do. Sometimes you have to take a call at 3:30 a.m. because you chose to live halfway around the world from all your contacts or fans. Is it worth it? Only you can answer that question.

When working with clients, you might also have to adjust your working hours so that you can respond to messages from them in a timely fashion. That doesn't mean you have to have a knee-jerk reaction to every incoming email or text, but you might, for example, set aside two hours early in the morning to check and respond to messages as well as an hour or two late at night to cover your bases.

As you travel among the different time zones of the world, keep in mind that you may also have to adjust your hours a little bit every time you move, depending on what kind of work you do and how often you have to interact with clients.

Celebrating the Rewards of the Digital Nomad Lifestyle

It's one thing to imagine why living a digital nomad lifestyle is rewarding and another to ask people who have done it. While everyone's reasons are personal, here are some reasons that digital nomads feel make the experience valuable.

Being Your Own Boss

Living in a country or city with a high cost of living can make it difficult to launch your own business or start a freelance career. When you travel to places with a much lower cost of living, however, it makes being your own boss a much more feasible prospect, as you don't have to earn nearly as much money to succeed. This gives you time to ease into your independent career path with less pressure.

Leaving the corporate world behind to explore your own career desire is a popular theme among digital nomads.

Freedom and Seeing the World

The location-independent lifestyle is rich with freedoms: the freedom to see the world by going where you want more or less when you want, and the freedom of having fewer obligations and responsibilities (no house or car to maintain, for example, and usually no boss to answer to).

When you don't commit to being anywhere for very long, you can stay as long as a place remains interesting or fulfilling and leave when you feel ready.

ALERT

Don't fool yourself into thinking that, as a digital nomad, you'll become a local. Visiting a new place for a few weeks or months has its rewards, and by staying longer than the average tourist, you will undoubtedly contribute more to the local economy. But it's not the same as living somewhere for years and settling into the culture.

This same sense of freedom or independence can have its downsides, however. If you're quick to leave a location as soon as it feels difficult, you miss out on some important aspects of the culture there.

The Minimalist's Life

Transient living means you have to pare down your belongings to what you can carry with you. A suitcase or two and a backpack are usually the extent of it. Living a more minimalistic life can be extremely rewarding for some, as their attitude shifts about the importance of "stuff."

A lot of digital nomads give up their possessions in phases. They may start by selling off major items, such as furniture and a car, but keep extra clothes, books, kitchen items, collectibles, and other effects in a storage unit or with friends during their first few journeys. When they come back to those items a few months or years later, it's common for digital nomads to see them as having less value, making it easier to give up more of them.

When digital nomads do stay in one location for a longer time, they might buy or acquire additional items for comfort, such as an office chair, computer monitor, more clothing, and so forth. Then they'll sell off or give away anything they can't keep when it's time to move. The secondhand market therefore becomes a valuable resource as digital nomads learn to reduce, reuse, and recycle.

How Digital Nomads Decide Where to Go

Deciding where to go as a digital nomad is an extremely personal process. There are a handful of common factors, however, that tend to influence the decision-making.

The question of where to go and how to decide is a popular topic of discussion, and you can easily learn a lot more about it by looking up blogs and online communities for digital nomads. Those discussions will also tip you off to a few popular regions, which include Southeast Asia, Eastern Europe, and some parts of Central America.

Interest

More than anything else, the desire to live and work in a place is driven by interest. It could be cultural interest and wanting to experience a place, or access to unique features, such as a great music scene, surfing, or world-class coffee.

Interests can also be simple preferences. What kind of weather do you like? Are you happy in a place that's far north or south on the globe and has extra hours of daylight a few months of the year? Maybe you want to live somewhere for its local food. Any of these interests and preferences, as well as infinite others, can and should influence where you go.

Low-Cost, High-Quality of Living

Very often digital nomads are on a quest for affordability. Where is the cost of living low but the quality of life still high?

One of the biggest costs for digital nomads is accommodations, so in addition to looking for overall low cost of living, it may be important to find an area that has plentiful short-term, furnished apartments and houses that rent at reasonable rates.

Internet Access, Reliability, and Speed

Without Internet access, most digital nomads couldn't work and make a living, so a location's Internet infrastructure is usually high on the list of factors when deciding where to go. More than just access, the Internet has to be reliable and reasonably fast. Trying to work in a location where short-term apartments typically come with only a hot spot for Internet service will be challenging, to say the least.

> **ESSENTIAL**
>
> There's a joke among digital nomads that they travel halfway around the world to end up in a Starbucks where the Wi-Fi is reliable. You have to do what you have to do for decent Wi-Fi, so be sure to pack a sense of humor.

Some workers might be able to get away with slower Internet speeds for the majority of their work, but it's still necessary for video calls, large file transfers, and a few other tasks that you may need to do.

Friendliness and Safety

How friendly is your intended destination to foreigners, outsiders, and tourists? Some places are not especially welcoming to transient workers. You might imagine you'll do just fine dealing with the occasional sideways look, but places that are unwelcoming can be more than just uncomfortable; they can be dangerous.

You wouldn't want to go to a place where no one will rent you an apartment, for example, or sell you basic necessities for a fair price. You might also consider the reputation of the police and whether they tend to harass, shake down, or cause harm to foreigners or people they perceive as different.

It's always advisable to educate yourself about how a particular society treats people based on race, religion, LGBTQ+ association, and other aspects of personal identity before deciding to go there.

Friends, Places to Stay

A rather simple way to choose a destination is to go where you know people. Having even a small network of friends, colleagues, or acquaintances in a new place can make it more fun to be there and easier to set up shop. Your friends will be there to help you navigate and learn the ins and outs of life on the ground.

Friends and other people in your network can also open up more opportunities when they need someone to house-sit or pet-sit. Working from someone else's home can be rather comfortable, too, if you know the right people.

Necessity

Every so often, a digital nomad might hightail it to a new location out of necessity. Some examples include family emergencies or celebrations, routine or emergency healthcare (there are many places in the world where you don't want to get a root canal), and electronic device repairs and replacements.

If you're looking to jump into digital nomad life for multiple years, you might want to think about and try to plan ahead for some of these necessities. For example, if you have to travel to your home country for a wedding, you might also schedule a dental cleaning and other preventive medical care appointments during that visit.

Being Aware of Visas and Location-Dependent Limitations

Before you set off to travel the world, it's really in your interest to make sure you know how to do it lawfully. The good news is that many countries have made it easy for remote workers to enter and work legally. It does take a little forethought and planning, however, which isn't always a strong suit for digital nomads.

The Tourist Visa (Avoid)

A troublesome truth about international digital nomads is that many of them enter on tourist visas and keep quiet about the fact that they're working while in the country. Most visas have strict rules, however, about whether you're allowed to work, and tourist visas are not work visas.

Depending on your passport and which country you're entering, a tourist visa could be free, available upon arrival, and require no paperwork whatsoever, other than a stamp in your passport. In other words, it's easy to get. If you're planning to work while in another country, though, this is not the right path. Don't do it.

Luckily, the world has started to understand remote work better, which means countries have an easier time developing policies and programs for remote workers. Many countries now offer visas that are specifically for remote workers who want to come and do their jobs from their shores. Most of them have an online application too. That makes getting the right permission easier and more convenient than in years past, so you have fewer excuses to not play by the rules.

Remote Work Visas

Remote work visas were somewhat unusual until the huge surge in remote work caused by the COVID-19 pandemic. Then, a number of countries started offering (or better promoting) visas for remote workers.

These visas make it relatively easy to know what the legal requirements are to live and work in a foreign country for an extended, but not permanent, period of time.

ALERT

Give yourself several weeks to learn about the details of the visa, apply for it, and wait for your approval or rejection. Some visa applications may require that you know what date you will arrive, although based on when the approval comes through, you may need to adjust it. Consider booking plane tickets with favorable change terms.

To give some generalized examples of countries offering visas for remote workers, quite a few places in the Caribbean do, including Barbados, Bermuda, Curaçao, and Dominica. There, a one-year or longer remote work visa is the norm. The application fees range from a few hundred dollars to a few thousand, and often you must prove that your annual salary meets the country's minimum requirement. After all, countries want some assurance that you can support yourself while you're there.

Europe, Estonia, Greece, Iceland, Romania, and a few additional countries offer digital nomad visas. Other European countries have other options for visas that similarly allow for longer visits while you work remotely, though they go by different names (e.g., independent contractor visa, self-employment work visa, long-stay visa, and so forth).

In addition to these countries, there are plenty of others all around the world that offer some kind of visa for remote workers.

ALERT

Applying for a visa is a strict process, so don't try to fudge it. If you do not meet the requirements exactly as they're written, you will lose your application fee and your visa will be denied. Make sure you can easily check all the boxes before applying.

The terms and application process for these visas vary by country, and the details of them can change at any time, so always check for the most recent information directly from the country or one of its embassies or consulates. Additionally, a country can remove a visa as an option at any time, so make sure you always refer to the most up-to-date information available.

Do Not Overstay Your Visa

Nearly all visas have a time limit on them. Make sure you know the exact date when your visa expires. Write it down in multiple places and create a reminder in your calendar or phone for a month before so it doesn't sneak up on you. Plan to leave the country before the expiration date. Overstaying your visa can put you in real trouble. You could be mandated to leave the country on very short notice.

If you need to extend your visa, be sure to find out if it's possible and learn what the process is well in advance of your visa expiration date.

Similarly, make sure you understand all the terms of your visa before you apply and after you receive it. There could be limitations on the number of times you enter and exit the country, for example.

Understanding Tax Implications and Health Insurance Issues

Not all digital nomads travel internationally. Within the United States, if you are a US taxpayer, you still have to be cognizant of where you go, how long you stay, and what you earned while there.

Additionally, your health insurance coverage may not go very far if you leave the state where you were a resident when you initially enrolled in your healthcare plan. The matter of health insurance can be a tricky subject for international travelers too.

State Taxes in the US

If in any given tax year you're planning to work from multiple US states, keep track of the dates you entered and exited each state, which days you worked, and what income you earned while there. You might not need this information, but if it turns out you do, you'll be glad you kept a record.

Living in a state, even for a few months, could technically make you a resident of that state. If you registered to vote, got a driver's license or state ID, enrolled your kids in school, or registered your vehicle there, you may have to file a tax return. The rules vary by state, so it's hard to say exactly what makes you a resident. You might also be considered a "statutory resident" of a state where you own a home, even if you don't currently live in it.

US state taxes are a royal pain when you have to calculate time spent in multiple states to pay the appropriate taxes there. Consider hiring a certified accountant to prepare your tax filings if you split time among states.

Health Insurance Coverage State by State

If you're employed full-time through a US employer and you have group health insurance coverage through your job, make sure you look up all the states where your coverage is accepted before traveling for an extended period of time in different states.

Not all health insurance plans have providers that they work with in all fifty states, not to mention the US territories. If you need medical care while you're bouncing from location to location, even if you never leave the US, you might have to get it from a provider that's outside your network, and that could drive up your medical bills considerably.

When planning a US-based digital nomad lifestyle with US employer-sponsored healthcare, be sure to check your coverage options thoroughly before you start moving around. If you need to adjust your coverage, you might have to wait for an open enrollment period and then wait another few months for the changes to take effect.

There's nothing preventing you from going to places where your healthcare coverage will be out of network, but it is important to know these risks and assess them appropriately before you go.

Health Insurance Coverage Abroad

For US travelers looking to go abroad while working, it's absolutely in your interest to review your healthcare coverage and potentially change it to a plan with adequate overseas coverage or purchase additional travel insurance to fill in major gaps in coverage.

It's also worth checking whether your plan includes emergency medical evacuation (medevac) coverage and repatriation of remains (meaning in the case of death, paying to transport your remains back to your home country). According to the US Department of State's travel information, very few health insurance companies cover medevacs, which can cost upward of $50,000, depending on your location and medical condition.

FACT

American Citizens Services and Crisis Management at any US embassy or consulate abroad can assist with some emergencies. Often on their websites you can find suggestions of local doctors and hospitals that have adequate facilities. Embassies and consulates specifically do not pay medical bills for citizens abroad, however.

Make sure you understand how your healthcare insurance works abroad, as well as any supplemental travel insurance policies you buy. For example, you may need to pay your overseas medical bills up front and then apply to get reimbursed by the plan later, often at out-of-network rates. Additionally, in some countries, hospitals require full payment of your bill before they will discharge you, so you may want to make sure you have access to liquid cash that you or a trusted friend can quickly wire in case of such an emergency.

Personal Risks and Trade-Offs for Digital Nomads

Exciting as it may seem to become a digital nomad, not having a home and living in unfamiliar places certainly creates unique risks. You'll also end up making some trade-offs to live the lifestyle.

Security and Safety

While digital nomads may take their personal safety into consideration when choosing a place to live temporarily, there are other safety-related concerns that come with living nomadically, such as increased risk of fraud (in certain countries and regions), online security, and so forth. Learning how to minimize risks and increase your safety takes time and mental resources, and you have to do it each time you move to a new location.

Learning a few tricks to increase your online safety is time well spent. Research which virtual private networks (VPNs) are right for your uses and then install them on all your devices. You might also want to set up automated alerts so you know when your credit and debit cards are used. While abroad, if you ever have to cancel and replace a bank card, you're in for an ordeal, as you'll need a secure address where the bank can send the card (consider staying at a nicer hotel for a night or two), and it could take a few days to reach you. You may also get charged for the fast international shipping needed to get the card into your hands quickly. Thankfully, this problem isn't quite as bad as it used to be because some banks can help you set up a virtual credit or debit card that you can use immediately via your smartphone when you make contactless payments, usually supported by Apple Wallet or Google Pay. That way you can still make payments while you're waiting for a new physical card to arrive. That said, if you're staying somewhere with a cash-based economy and are waiting on a replacement ATM card, a virtual card isn't going to help.

QUESTION

Why do I need to be more concerned about online privacy as a digital nomad?
You should always be concerned with online privacy no matter where you are. When traveling, however, you're never the administrator of any Wi-Fi network you use. Anytime you connect to a network that you don't administer, anyone could be accessing your traffic. Additionally, credit card skimming and other financial crimes are much higher in some countries than in others.

There are also matters of personal safety that vary from place to place. Educate yourself on the safety and crime of each place you stay. Add to your phone the local numbers for ambulance, police assistance, the fire department, and other emergency information.

Doing all these little tasks can start to sap your mental resources. Moving from place to place isn't just physically tiring; it's also mentally tiring. Staying vigilant about your personal and online safety takes up space in your cognitive load.

Lack of Community, Meaningful Relationships

In the digital nomad lifestyle, you will likely connect with other digital nomads as well as different kinds of long-term travelers. They can be wonderful resources for learning how to navigate all the places you visit.

By and large, however, they'll be acquaintances you meet along the way and not real friends. When no one stays in any given place for long, it's rare to develop a lasting community or deep friendships.

You'll also have to deal with the fact that your friends and family members from your former home all continue their lives without you. It's tough to keep those relationships strong when you aren't physically available to be with people when they need you, see their children grow up, celebrate milestones, or enjoy life's simple pleasures together.

Loneliness

Living without a strong community or deep friendships can get lonely, especially for digital nomads who live and travel solo.

You might assume that as you galivant through the world, you can always go out and meet people, but the reality is that natural disasters and other unexpected events (protests or civil unrest, disease outbreaks, mass shootings, the odd coup d'état) can lead you to be alone for days at a time or longer.

Family, Pets, and Putting Down Roots

When you choose to move regularly and not settle down, you necessarily give up some of your options related to family life. Plus, all the time that you travel, you are necessarily not putting down roots anywhere. It's perfectly fine to not want these things in life, but it's also useful to acknowledge that you're giving them up.

While some digital nomads travel with partners and children, it is difficult. Figuring out how and where to educate kids is a big consideration. Homeschooling takes a lot of effort, energy, and time. Local schools are an option, but you'll have to consider how often you'll move and yank your kids away from their learning path, friendships, and ability to pick up the local language if it's new to them.

While there are tales of digital nomads who have pets, it is difficult, time-consuming, and expensive to take pets across borders. Figuring out the country-to-country requirements for importing pets is stressful too. Proving your pet has the right vaccination records, health certificates, and other paperwork is challenging. There's a lot that goes into taking care of an animal while traveling internationally, and there's a reason most digital nomads don't have pets.

Other Lifestyle Trade-Offs

There are numerous other lifestyle trade-offs you make to live as a digital nomad. Your wardrobe won't be extravagant, so don't expect to pull the right outfit out of your suitcase for every occasion. It's not impossible to own a property while living nomadically, but you'll need a property manager and healthy reserve funds in case it sits unrented or needs significant repairs.

Many digital nomads embrace minimalism by selling off or giving away their belongings. Renouncing all worldly possessions for the long term doesn't suit everyone. If you're a collector or have prized items, you'll need a place to store them and will have to think about how long that can last. Two or three years of storage unit payments can easily add up to more than the value of the items you're saving for some theoretical future life when you settle down in one place again.

Case Study: The Cognitive Cost of Being a Digital Nomad

For about a decade, Dave Dean was a digital nomad. He left a well-paying job in the corporate world to become an online entrepreneur, promising himself that if he could earn $1,000 a month, he could go live in Thailand. He did.

From there, he traveled the world at a clip, sometimes moving to a new country every few days. After four or five years, however, he realized he wasn't making significantly more money compared to when he started. "I wasn't getting there while traveling full-time, partially because of the cognitive load of traveling and the physical load of doing it. It's pretty hard to focus on anything for more than two or three weeks at a time," he said.

Eventually he slowed down. "I needed to be stopped for a lot longer if I was ever going to really ramp up my business," Dean says. He and his partner chose Lisbon, Portugal, and made it a home base. He continued traveling but now had somewhere to go when his mind needed to rest from making travel plans and instead focus on work. A year or so after that, his business improved dramatically. Since then, he's moved a few more times but much more slowly. He says living a location-independent lifestyle benefited him hugely, even if he now stays in one spot a lot longer.

Professional Risks and Trade-Offs for Digital Nomads

Professionally speaking, you'll take some risks and make some trade-offs as a digital nomad too. As mentioned, very few digital nomads are employed by organizations. Most are independent freelancers, contractors, or entrepreneurs. No matter where you are in the world, there is no promotion or career advancement track when you're independent, aside from the one you create for yourself.

Lower Income

Some digital nomads earn a lower income, especially when they're first starting out, compared to what they would have earned if they took a full-time job in their career in their home country and stayed put.

There's nothing wrong with having a lower income, particularly when you choose to live in a place with a lower cost of living. In fact, your lifestyle may actually improve. However, if you have existing debt that you're trying to pay off, the amount you earn affects how quickly you can get rid of it. That in turn affects your savings, which affects your ability to invest or purchase property later on, and so forth.

So while it may seem fine to accept a lower income for the foreseeable future, it could have additional consequences for you later. Keep that in mind.

Lack of a Plan

The freedom of the digital nomad lifestyle means you often operate without much of a plan. You remain flexible and open to adjusting where you are and what you might do next based on the conditions on the ground.

The negative side of this freedom is that you essentially operate without a plan, and without a plan, it's very hard to have midrange and long-term goals related to your career or profession and make significant progress toward them.

Limitations on Opportunities

Depending on what kind of work you do, there may be missed opportunities or limitations on professional opportunities due to the fact that you don't have a fixed home.

For example, when an organization is vetting contractors or freelancers for long-term relationships, they sometimes invite them to meet in person. That can be tough if you're living out of a suitcase in Ho Chi Minh City and the client is in Louisiana. Based on the work that needs to be done, they may also want the contractor to be able to be on-site with very short notice. If you're halfway around the world, it could take that long just to get the message and reply to the client, much less wait for them to buy you a $5,000 flight. Some clients prefer to do business with contractors who are at their beck and call.

If your industry has important trade shows or conferences, will you be able to attend them? Can you afford to get to the location where they're held and stay for a few days?

As much as you may feel like you have complete freedom and mobility to go where you want when you want, the logistics of getting to a particular destination for an event aren't always simple, straightforward, or cheap.

CHAPTER 13

How to Participate in Remote Company Culture

Remote organizations rely on employees to help build and sustain the organizational or company culture. It's not all top-down. In a remote setting, employees have to take a more active role in making sure the culture gives them what they want and need because unlike in-person workplaces, there isn't much opportunity for spontaneity. You have to decide what you want from your work environment and relationships, and then make it happen.

Contributing to Company Culture As a Remote Employee

Every person in an organization shapes the culture for better or worse. Some do it through active participation in social events, while others may refrain from any interaction beyond their job function, keeping the culture more impersonal. In remote workplaces, it's important for you and your colleagues to be aware of how you influence the culture so it can be what you want it to be.

FACT

Organizational culture, or company culture, refers to the attitudes and behaviors of a business. Essentially, it's the style and feel of the workplace: formal or informal, high-stress or laid-back, friendly or straitlaced, and so on. The culture stems from not only the organization's policies and procedures but also how employees interact and any additional activities they create.

Remote employees drive much of the organizational culture as it relates to socializing (although the rest predominately comes from the top down). As a remote employee, you and your coworkers set your level of comfort for interacting with one another about both work and nonwork-related matters. You decide how formal or informal you want to be, whether you want to develop friendships at work or beyond working hours, and so forth. Significant influence still comes from the top regarding the mission statement of the business, values, and some matters of policy, but you really do have a strong role in shaping the social culture and mood overall. Nearly all nonwork or work-adjacent activities, such as virtual happy hours, book club groups, or regional in-person meetups, are created and run by you and your peers.

Culture also plays a major role in whether people work long hours and are susceptible to burnout. Management and leadership undoubtedly lay the groundwork in this area, but in remote work, it's also up to you and your colleagues to not drive yourselves toward burnout by working excessively. It's tricky to demonstrate that you're putting in adequate effort to do your job while also taking care of yourself and your needs, which can sometimes mean pushing back on work. Funnily enough, a great way to gauge whether you're putting in adequate effort and balancing your life appropriately is to socialize with coworkers: Get to know them better, learn more about how they find good work–personal life balance while working remotely, and find out if they have any problematic relationships with other coworkers or managers.

> **FACT**
>
> Organizational culture has an effect on employee engagement, which in turn affects employee retention (whether you stick around or look for another job). In a 2020 Nielsen survey, 65 percent of experienced remote workers said they were very or somewhat engaged, with a scant 2 percent saying they felt disengaged.

Why is organizational culture important? It affects employee morale, team cohesion and how well people work together, as well as whether you find your job fulfilling. Being in an organization where the culture suits you makes the act of working a more pleasant experience.

Strengthening Relationships

A big component to remote work culture has to do with how much you socialize with other employees.

At in-person workplaces, you'll often find groups of people who have lunch together regularly, socialize after work hours, or even volunteer together for a cause. But in remote workplaces, those kinds of get-togethers take more effort and coordination, even if they're virtual. You can't spontaneously ask whoever is within earshot if they want to share a pizza. You have to actively reach out to people.

Socializing can help strengthen relationships, which in turn makes it easier to communicate with people (there are some ideas on how to do it in the next sections). The more you get to know your colleagues, the easier it is to understand their tone of voice in written communication, as well as know how to best work with them.

For example, if you learn that a particular coworker likes very direct and clear feedback and doesn't tend to take feedback personally, you may learn to use a very different communication style with them compared with other people who, for example, might not have high confidence in their work. It's wonderful when coworkers know themselves well enough to share this information with you transparently, but not everyone is so self-aware. Socializing and interacting with people informs your understanding of who they are.

Likewise, as you get to know people and understand them better, you might have different expectations for how they go about working. Some people have a slow and steady approach to meeting deadlines, for example, while others work best when they get their work done very close to when it's due. Getting to know these little differences allows you to have a clearer sense of when work is going smoothly and when there's a potential problem.

Building Trust

When you know how people work best, it gives you greater confidence in their ability to get their job done, even when they work differently from you. The quickest way to know how people work best is to get to know them.

The combination of getting to know people and experiencing how they work firsthand (e.g., learning that not only do they say they work best on a short deadline, but also witnessing that they do indeed come through in the end) helps to build trust. And when trust is high, people work together well.

Keeping Morale High

When teammates get to know each other, it can keep morale high and foster more empathy among them.

In remote work, not knowing one of your teammates well can turn them into something of a black box. When you don't see someone in person and you only interact with them in virtual meetings and via asynchronous communication, there's a lot of information missing that turns someone from merely a name into a fully formed person. Working with people, as opposed to black boxes, can boost morale.

Morale among employees often starts from the state of the business and how the leadership team projects itself (unless there are serious interpersonal conflicts or problematic people, and then it's usually rooted there). There are other ways employees contribute to morale, however. Celebrating team successes, providing positive feedback, and just generally being cheery in your written communication keep people's spirits high.

Making It Fun, Making It Optional

When coming up with new activities, events, or ideas that add to the organizational culture, always try to make them fun while also making sure participation is truly optional.

Step Up and Create Your Own Events or Activities

In remote organizations, and especially among teams that are larger than just a few people, it's nice to have social events on offer for those who want them. Your employer might create some, but many will be homegrown. So if there's something you want to see, take initiative and create it.

Not all events and activities require a mountain of up-front work. Sure, quiz nights and book clubs need a person to run them, but you can also inject fun, happiness, and camaraderie through small, everyday acts. For example, some remote teams have sporadic virtual dance parties, where everyone in a team chat channel posts an animated GIF or emoji for a few minutes, just to break up the monotony of the day. Or you could share a fun fact once a week related to a coworker's hobby or the place where they live or are from.

If you do want to create an activity that requires some amount of planning and organization, consider partnering with a colleague or two so that the burden isn't all on you.

Don't Make It about Work

A quiz about baby animals is fun. A quiz about company policies or who had the best sales figures last quarter is just more work disguised as fun. If you're trying to make work a happier place to be and boost morale, don't make your activities and events about work.

When people participate in something extracurricular, they want to connect with their coworkers and give their minds some rest while doing something enjoyable. They don't want to learn about the history of the company's logo.

It Must Be Truly Optional

Events and activities meant to make work a happier place do not, in fact, make work a happier place for everyone. Some people find them tedious or grating or a waste of time that they'd rather spend doing something else. And they have every right to feel that way and not participate. Some remote workers get into remote work so that they can spend less time at work and more time enjoying their personal life.

Every "fun" event at work should be truly optional, meaning people who don't join aren't affected negatively for their lack of participation. That may sound straightforward, but getting it right requires some subtlety. For example, if one person routinely does not participate in extra activities while everyone else does, the loner starts to stand out. If inside jokes develop, they're not a part of them. If team cohesion strengthens among everyone except this one person, the result won't be good. The team may have to adjust to focus on strengthening cohesion within the context of work rather than through supposedly optional activities.

Another option that some remote companies do is ask everyone to share publicly something from their personal life on a regular basis, such as habits they're trying to form or what they did on the weekend. It may seem like an activity to foster connection, but if it's not done on an opt-in basis, it can also feel like you're being forced into revealing more about your private life than you feel comfortable doing.

QUESTION

What if an activity doesn't feel truly optional?
Pass along that feedback to your manager or the organizer of the activity. If people have to opt out rather than opt in, that's reason enough for some kindly worded feedback. Or, identify why it doesn't feel optional and take your time to phrase the feedback in a way that isn't personal.

Volunteer efforts and raising money for charity is another area where supposedly optional participation can start to feel mandatory. In remote work, a lot of these activities take place online in public spaces, meaning everyone can see who has contributed, and that can create significant peer pressure. Always keep in mind that not everyone wants to or can participate. How will they feel or be perceived by others if they don't? Keep these points in mind when coming up with activities and events.

Socializing with Colleagues

Everyday conversations with colleagues don't just happen in remote work. You have to make them happen. Remote organizations usually provide employees with a couple of outlets for socializing. That said, participating in the social aspects of work is optional, not mandatory. You can skip them if you're not interested.

Social Channels

One of the primary ways people socialize at work on a day-to-day, hour-to-hour basis is in the social channels within the organization's team messaging app (such as Slack and Microsoft Teams). These socializing channels are so important to teams that Slack even gives you one by default (#watercooler) when you first set up the app. The idea is to give everyone a place to chitchat informally at work, the way you might around a watercooler in an office.

Most remote organizations create many more channels for fun and socializing, and you should feel encouraged to not only join them but also to create your own based on your interests or topics you enjoy discussing.

Parenting, pets, news, sports, television, women and women's issues, and the LGBTQ+ community are common social channel themes. There might also be groups for people who are dealing with specific illnesses, such as cancer or chronic pain. When multiple employees are in the same geographic region, there are sometimes groups for them to discuss local issues, and occasionally organize meetups.

Direct Messages and Other Private Conversations

When it comes to fostering friendships and business relationships one-on-one, you can largely do it through direct messages at a remote job. In this context, direct messages are almost always going to take place in a team messaging app. There, you can have private, ongoing conversations with one or a few people.

Do use direct messages to check in on people. Ask how they're doing. See whether they understood the announcements in the last all-hands meeting. It's a really simple way to show that you're thinking about another person and are making an effort to build rapport with them.

ALERT

Private work chats are never truly private. Any conversations you have with other employees on official company software, including team messaging apps, email, and video conferencing apps, are accessible to the administrators, meaning whoever manages the apps. Never have conversations using work software that you wouldn't want your boss or anyone else at the organization to see.

Consider the People You're Not Socializing With

In a physical workplace, you may have had coworkers who come off as grumpy, irritated, and unsociable. (Or you could have been that coworker.) Saying "Good morning!" to someone who doesn't always return the greeting can make work feel uncomfortable. In remote work, all those people who don't interact easily with others or don't enjoy it don't have to. That means you don't have to either.

You can send a message to someone in your organization who seems shy or whom you haven't met and ask how they're doing or if they want to chat more sometime, but don't push it. There are remote workers who are happiest when left alone. If someone shows signs that they're not interested in socializing or developing a relationship, consider yourself lucky for not having to have awkward, daily in-person encounters with them.

Re-Creating "Watercooler" Moments Virtually

One unique challenge of remote work is that when you're virtual, you never bump into someone in a hallway or at the watercooler. Some people talk about these kinds of chance encounters as having a mythical air. Every industry has some legend of a watercooler moment that has led to a multimillion-dollar product or some breakthrough idea. Regardless of the lore, some people simply like watercooler moments. So why not re-create this feeling of chance encounter in a remote workplace?

As mentioned previously, team chat apps often include a #watercooler channel where people can chat informally about nonwork topics. It doesn't quite capture the happenstance nature of bumping into someone at the watercooler, but there are plug-ins for team chat apps that do.

Donut Calls

The Donut plug-in for Slack is one of the most popular plug-ins for the platform. It randomly pairs up two or more people in the organization and invites them to talk for a few minutes at a time that they arrange. Whoever administers the plug-in can choose how many people to match up and how often to do it. (If you don't like to futz around with plug-ins, it isn't too hard to run a similar program and pair people up manually, as long as the head count isn't astronomical.)

Some organizations have an informal rule that Donut chats should be about nonwork topics. That way, you get to know people beyond just their job titles and functions.

Remember, these types of programs should be rolled out on an opt-in basis. In other words, you should have to elect yourself into them rather than excuse yourself from participating if you don't want to.

Cross-Team Chats

When you first join a remote organization, your manager might suggest you reach out to a few key people in different departments to get to know who they are, what they do, how their team contributes to the organization, and so forth.

There's no reason to limit yourself to only learning about other departments and employees when you're new, however. If someone's name comes up while discussing a project or in a meeting and you don't know much about that person or what they do, there's nothing wrong with sending a private message and asking if they would like to have a virtual coffee sometime. Be clear why you're reaching out (in other words, the context in which you stumbled on their name) and ask to keep it short: Ten minutes is plenty. Not everyone will be into it, but not everyone is keen on making chitchat at a physical watercooler either.

Even if you don't think you would enjoy virtual watercooler meetings, give them a try two or three times. That way, you'll know for sure what they are, rather than relying on your own assumptions, and you'll have an experience with more than one person before you choose not to do it again in the future.

Getting What You Need from Team Retreats and Business Travel

In terms of organizational culture, the little in-person time you do get with colleagues at retreats and through other business travel can be foundational. As much as possible, you should try to think ahead and make some plans that allow you to get what you need during the time you're together.

FACT

According to a 2021 report from PwC, 87 percent of employees say having an office is important for collaborating and building relationships. When you don't have an office, retreats and other in-person gatherings are your next best bet.

Time with Your Team and Teammates

Someone will organize a team meal on a retreat. Someone will book time for a team meeting or two. Are those planned get-togethers enough for you to feel like you know your colleagues and will have a better relationship with them after the retreat is over?

Ask yourself whether you do best in groups or whether you're better at building relationships when you're one-on-one with individuals. You might get more out of a retreat by planning several one-on-one moments than by spending all your time in a group.

> **ESSENTIAL**
>
> Another very good reason to spend one-on-one time with your peers is to discuss work-related issues that you don't want recorded or potentially captured by work software. Delicate issues, such as rocky interpersonal relationships or problems with management, are often best shared in person. Some candid information you will only get face-to-face.

Time with Your Manager and Leadership

At any retreat, you'll spend some time with your manager in both groups and one on one. As mentioned previously, it's always beneficial to take a moment to say hello in person to founders, executives, or other people on the leadership team while you're in the same physical location as well. These interactions aren't just for the sake of making sure people know who you are. They're also for you to get a stronger sense of what the organizational culture is from their perspective.

Leaders in the organization should have a clear message that they communicate frequently to employees regarding the mission statement and vision, but sometimes it's nice to hear what they think unscripted. What do they think is going well? What are they actively trying to improve? How far into the future do they think? Are they considering any pivots or adjustments to how they approach the business due to market changes or other external factors?

Your manager could also be more open to speaking in an unscripted and more candid fashion when you're one-on-one in person, just as your teammates might.

After a retreat, when everyone heads back to their remote work setup, you may have a much clearer and richer understanding of the organizational culture based on your experiences. Hopefully it's mostly positive and the mood can carry forward until the next time you're face-to-face again.

Time to Observe the Vibe

A valuable exercise at a retreat is to remove yourself from the hubbub and simply observe. Who are the extroverts? Who tends to congregate in groups? What topics make people's faces light up? During downtime, what do people like to do outside of the retreat programming? What's the general vibe?

By observing how other people interact, what their interests are, who's good at taking charge of a situation, and other traits and behaviors, you can learn a lot about the culture. You can also start to see people's strengths and weaknesses, which can help you make better decisions at work related to how you collaborate.

Organizing Regional Meetups, Online Meetups, and Clubs

Any meetups and clubs that are offered at your workplace will almost certainly be created and run by employees. It's one of the areas where you can contribute most to the remote work culture, but only if you want to.

Meetups and clubs are ideal for people who like making friends through work and feel most comfortable doing it within the bounds of an organized activity. Because remote work environments lack spontaneity, you're unlikely to make friends by chance. You have to be more proactive in creating opportunities to make friends at work (again, only if you want them in the first place).

Regional Meetups

It's not unusual for several people in a remote organization to live in the same region, seeing as many industries have hot spots of talent. When that's the case, regional in-person meetups are a great way to get to know some of your coworkers better and open the possibility of making new local friends. Meetups can be as simple as a group coffee outing or lunch a few times a year, or an organized activity, such as a group hike, dog or kid playdate, or visit to a local site or museum.

You can also have regional meetups when you travel to a place where several colleagues live, or when they travel to a place near you.

Remember, all these types of get-togethers should be optional. If you're the person who suggests them, make sure you invite people in such a way that they must opt in rather than opt out.

Online Meetups

Online meetups are virtual meetings held for fun rather than for work. You can have meetups that mirror activities you could do in the real world, like happy hours or lunches, or something that's unique to being online.

When organizing online meetups, be aware of people's time zones. It might be impossible to host a virtual lunch for your colleagues in Australia, Israel, and California at the same time, but perhaps suggest that the next one will be at a different time to make it easier for different people to join. If you're dedicated to making online meetups a social activity for you and your colleagues, you might have to be the one who joins at an inconvenient time of day to make it happen.

Clubs

Clubs are similar to online meetups except that they tend to attract a regular group of members. As a result, clubs are a nice way to form tighter bonds with a select few people. Just as with meetups, clubs can be regionally based and held in person, but more commonly they're online and therefore open to everyone in the organization to join.

Book clubs are one of the most popular types of clubs you'll find in remote work, perhaps because like remote work, they can be done asynchronously. You can have a synchronous video meeting to discuss a book, of course, and you can have an asynchronous chat where people discuss it, too, making the conversation accessible to people who can't or don't want to join yet another video call.

Other types of clubs you might consider creating are game night or trivia, or even a tasting party where everyone tries to buy the same food or beverage items (or you can buy them in bulk and ship out samples) in advance. Fitness clubs, especially group yoga, tend to be popular in remote work as well.

Celebrating Successes and Boosting Morale

Positive organizational cultures celebrate successes, both individual and team-based, and take care to carve out other moments for boosting morale.

When successes aren't celebrated, especially in remote work, it can start to feel like you're in a vacuum. Your work may seem devoid of meaning if no one appreciates that you do it. You want to know that your contributions matter.

Remote work offers plenty of ways to celebrate others and your team for a job well done.

Little Everyday Celebrations

When you and all your coworkers are in the middle of a grueling work-day, it's a nice surprise to pop into one of the team chat channels and see a virtual dance party, where everyone posts an animated GIF or emoji during a few minutes of silliness.

Remote workers sometimes have similar online "parties" in honor of someone's birthday or a milestone: running their first marathon, getting married, being quoted by a major news outlet, and so forth.

Finding appropriate ways to take a short break—reminding yourself and everyone else that work isn't always super serious—and experience a little camaraderie can make people feel good.

Positive Feedback

It's hard to overstate how meaningful positive feedback is for people, including when it comes from their peers with no implications about a possible future promotion or wage increase—just pure "you did a great job, and I noticed."

It feels good when someone recognizes the work that you do. You can give people that same good feeling by sharing positive feedback regularly.

Feedback, both corrective and positive, should always be a part of remote business culture, and its endurance depends in part on you and your colleagues giving it, not merely waiting for others to give it to you.

So strengthen the role of positive feedback in your organizational culture by giving it often. Twice a month is a good target if you're new to it. Always give feedback that's specific, relevant, and clear. Look at what people bring to their roles or the team that's exceptional or unique, and say how or why it has a positive effect.

> **QUESTION**
>
> **In hybrid-remote work, should I wait until I'm face-to-face with someone to give them positive feedback?**
> Nope! There's never a reason to delay positive feedback when you're working with a remote-first mindset. When someone does something great, tell them. The considerations for corrective feedback, however, are different.

Do some people hear this model for feedback and say it sounds forced and is therefore less compelling? Yes, it happens. If it feels a bit much, start with very simple positive feedback, like "That was a great comment" or "Thank you for doing/saying…"

Care Packages and Tokens of Appreciation

Some remote teams like to celebrate a success or boost morale with a care package activity. The idea is for someone on the team (it's usually the manager, so go ahead and suggest this to your manager if they've never done it) to deliver something physical to all team members at roughly the same time, and then everyone enjoys whatever it is together on a video call.

For example, if all the team members are roughly in the same time zone, the manager might arrange for everyone to get a pizza delivery, and then you can have a virtual team pizza lunch. For less time-sensitive deliveries, it could be shelf-stable treats, or a nonperishable gift such as a book, a mug, bath bombs, or whatever else the team might enjoy.

In remote work, where there are never bagels in the communal kitchen or cake for someone's birthday, unexpected gifts and other tokens of appreciation can boost morale and help people feel recognized for their work.

Surprise Time Off

Another way to celebrate and recognize good work is to give people surprise time off (again, it has to come from management, but there's no reason you can't suggest it). Getting a half-day Friday or a surprise long weekend is especially nice if the team or organization has recently been through intense work periods or stress.

Surprise time off isn't as effective if it's a real short-term surprise because then people can't plan for and make the most of their time. It's much more appreciated when people get at least a week's notice.

All these various ways of celebrating and rewarding one another make the business culture more fun and keep morale high.

Employee Perks Commonly Offered at All-Remote Companies

Employee perks and benefits contribute to organizational culture too. When they're done right, they send the message that someone has actually gone to some length to think about what you as an employee need to feel recognized, happy, and productive.

Remote workers miss out on little perks of being in a physical workspace, like complimentary coffee, tea, and snacks, or the occasional breakfast spread or celebratory cake. There are no giveaways of holiday swag in remote work, no office gym, no on-site childcare. While remote workers have a lot going for them in exchange (no commute, no commuting expenses, no need to have a full business-appropriate wardrobe, etc.), it adds to the positive work culture when the employer offers other perks to make up for what employees are missing from an in-person experience.

Discounts on Coffee, Snacks, and Meal Subscriptions

To make up for the lack of snacks, some remote employers offer a special employee discount on subscription services for coffee to brew at home, meal kits or prepared meals, and other food items.

There are some troubles with these types of perks, however. If the subscription on offer doesn't fit with your dietary needs, you might feel short-changed. The same goes for people who are located outside the service zone.

To make it more equitable, some employers might offer a range of options to make sure there's something for everyone. Ultimately, however, not all little perks are 100 percent equitable. Would you have complained about getting shortchanged if you never drank the complimentary coffee at an office?

Coworking Space Stipends

Because working from home isn't the right fit for every remote worker, some companies offset or fully reimburse the cost of a coworking space for those who need it. Occasionally, companies offer some kind of reimbursement program for people who don't need a coworking space membership full time but do need to go somewhere else from time to time, such as a short-term office space rental or even expensing a few dollars a month at a coffee shop while working.

Paid Sabbaticals

Sabbaticals—which are exceedingly rare in US institutions, except academia—are meant to be an extended break from work when a person can pursue other interests that they may not normally be able to do while working. It's a generous benefit, which remote organizations need to offer if they want to attract the top talent available worldwide.

A few well-known remote-first organizations offer paid sabbaticals. For example, the all-remote company Buffer gives employees six weeks off, fully paid, every five years; and Automattic encourages employees to take up to three months off every five years.

In academia, professors and lecturers who get sabbaticals are often strongly encouraged to research, write, and publish without the usual work of a semester's course load, sometimes with an expectation of what kind of work they'll produce on their sabbatical. In other sectors, workers can use the paid time off however they want, although it's a unique opportunity to spend time doing something that's difficult to do while you're working.

Case Study: What Do People Do on Sabbatical?

Automattic, the company behind WordPress.com, *Tumblr*, *Longreads*, and other brands, is an all-remote company that offers a paid sabbatical as part of its employee benefits.

On its employee benefits page, the company highlights blog posts written by a few employees as they were planning or after they took their sabbaticals. Most wanted time for travel. As a remote worker, you can always travel, but you can't always travel without working. On sabbatical, you can. Most Automattic employees also said they needed time to simply rest. A few turned to hobbies and activities that fell out of practice, such as playing guitar, volunteering, and taking dance and yoga classes. By reading about what remote employees did with their sabbaticals, you can get a sense of what's difficult to do when working remotely full-time.

Education Programs and Learning Stipends

A generous employee perk sometimes found in both remote and location-based workplaces is for the employer to pay tuition for any employee who wants to get an accredited degree. It's not too common, but it's a great benefit when it's available and you can take advantage of it.

Better are remote organizations that pay for degree programs *and* other kinds of learning that don't necessarily result in a degree. For example, some organizations offer learning stipends or reimbursement for books, audio books, non-degree courses, podcast subscriptions, and other kinds of personal enrichment, despite whether it's directly related to your job.

CHAPTER 14

Preparing for the Future of Remote Work

The future of work undoubtedly will include more remote work, and the future of remote work rests on flexibility. In the immediate future, you have to be flexible while organizations and the people who work at them learn how to work remotely more effectively. No one gets it right from the start, and some will never get it entirely right. You also have to be flexible as conditions change, as employers try out new configurations, and as you change your mind about what you want from a remote work lifestyle.

Turning Toward a Remote-Inclusive Mindset

In the coming years, remote work will be different from flexwork of the past. Flexwork was always predicated on having a fixed location where the majority of people worked five days a week in person together. That antiquated vision was built on the assumption that work is done best when done in person. Now, however, there's plenty of evidence that people can do their best work from anywhere.

Remote work today and into the future has to be built on more up-to-date assumptions, data, and learned best practices. Additionally, workplaces have to be designed to support remote work, and you have to feel like you're a part of the process and have agency.

Just as important, every individual worker, including you, can do their part to learn about remote work and contribute to making it better for not only yourself, but also your coworkers, clients, colleagues, managers, and everyone else in your world of work.

Why Remote-First?

The remote-first approach to work says businesses should build their policies, processes, and culture with the intention to support remote work by default. A workplace that supports remote work can also accommodate in-person work just fine, but a system built around in-person work doesn't always support remote work equally. In other words, the remote-first approach takes a stance of "leave no one behind." It's a way of making sure everyone is included no matter where or when they work.

Generally speaking, the remote-first mindset is an all-around more contemporary way to approach business because it gets rid of old assumptions about work that were established long before the invention of many technologies available today. For example, a lot of old assumptions about the need for meetings come from an era before email, team chat apps, collaborative online documents, and cloud-based software. Those assumptions were rooted in the idea that people had to be physically present in a room together to have a discussion and make business decisions in a timely fashion.

None of that is true anymore. Meetings do still have a role in business in a remote-first environment, but the need for them and their purpose can be based on more up-to-date assumptions.

The remote-first approach also welcomes globalization. When businesses aren't limited to hiring people from select geographic areas, they have a larger pool of talent to draw from and can therefore attract top talent. That also means businesses are competing with one another to hire that top talent. For you, that means potentially tough competition when you're a job candidate, but it also means employers offer attractive compensation packages to woo you over, from competitive pay to sabbaticals.

Remote Work Must Be a Choice

Catastrophes aside, you should be able to choose remote work, not be forced into it. In the same way you might accept or reject a job offer for an in-person role based on the location and commute, the terms of remote work should be defined in such a way that you have agency in choosing whether you will partake in it. This means employers have to be clear about what options they're going to present to current or future employees, which you then accept, reject, or negotiate. You need to know what you're agreeing to.

The fact that you can choose to work remotely full-time, part-time, or not at all gives you agency, and having agency usually makes for happier employees. That increased happiness has positive effects on your productivity, loyalty, and other traits that are good for both you and your employer. It's also just a better way to live.

Plan and Design for the Future

Going remote without a plan doesn't work. You can't take a business that used to be done in person, move it online, and expect everything to still work the same. When preparing for a future that includes remote work, businesses have to design and plan for it. They need to be intentional about the policies, procedures, and tools used in the workplace to set you up for success. It's really hard to overstate the importance of designing and planning for remote work.

Thankfully, there are some remote-first organizations that have been finessing their remote work practices since well before the COVID-19 pandemic, and they can be valuable resources for everyone else. They've figured out how to prioritize asynchronous work, treat meetings as precious and rare time together, and organize retreats and other gatherings to give everyone some valuable in-person time too.

Organizations and employees should be open to learning from their example while also adapting and adjusting their practices as they work remotely and figure out what works and what doesn't. There is no blueprint for supporting remote work that works perfectly for every organization, but there are a lot of best practices supported by data that can steer everyone in the right direction.

Flexibility

Here's a reality about the future of remote work: Most organizations haven't offered remote work to any real extent in the past and are still learning how to do it. The same goes for workers. As a result, everyone has to be flexible moving into a future where remote work is more commonplace.

Flexibility relates to not only the logistics and management practices of remote work but also to how you and other employees feel about it. If you're already part of a workforce that's transitioning into a new remote situation, your whole organization might go through different stages while collecting feedback about how well it's working. What remote work is could change between the first quarter and the fourth, based on people's reactions to it. Be prepared for some amount of instability.

FACT

In the past, attitudes about remote work have swung from one extreme to the other. Large organizations, including IBM and Yahoo!, for years had generous policies about remote work, but they later reversed course and took away the option entirely. If the future is anything like the past, these same shifts may happen again.

Likewise, how you feel about being remote could change over time. As much as possible, leave yourself room to make changes. For example, you might at first believe that you'd like a hybrid schedule, but after a few weeks of going to a half-empty office, you realize it's not what you thought it would be. Make sure you and your boss are ready to adjust to these changes. As much as possible, don't lock yourself into a long-term commitment. Discuss the option to try out a particular remote work setup for, say, three months and then evaluate whether it's working well.

Supporting Remote Options

For remote work to work, employers have to know what options they're willing to offer, and you have to know what's possible so you can negotiate those options. Even a full-time remote job has room for negotiation, such as which hours you make yourself available to collaborate in real time and how often you participate in business travel and retreats.

No matter what kind of agreement you land on, you need to feel supported in your remote setup.

Feeling Informed and Included

To reiterate a previous point because it is crucial, remote work should be a situation you opt in to. Whether you accept a job offer that was advertised as remote or you coordinate with your boss to come up with a hybrid schedule that both of you can agree on, you have to be a part of the decision-making process. You must be informed and included all along the way.

FACT

Feeling clued in to the plans for remote work at your organization matters for your performance. According to a 2021 McKinsey & Company report, when employees felt included in receiving detailed communication about how their employer would handle remote work options in the near future, they were nearly five times more likely to report being more productive.

Getting the Support You Deserve

In taking a remote-first approach to work, employers make a commitment to support employees as they work remotely. This means supplying you with physical equipment and furniture, software, training, and managerial support, as well as advice and guidance when appropriate.

It also means communicating to you clearly what going remote means, along with all the expectations the organization has, such as what hours you need to be available or the expected turnaround time for answering email. You deserve to work in conditions where all these details are clear. Organizations that are new to remote work may not have figured them all out yet, but it's certainly within your rights to ask and perhaps even steer the leadership team into considering some points they may have overlooked related to remote work policies.

A good, future-leaning, remote-first workplace should be supportive on a human level too. Managers should adjust to your needs (and vice versa). Colleagues can be a source of support and joy. It's up to you to build relationships, create opportunities to socialize, and learn more about what's happening at work by interacting with people as you see fit. If you're happier to not socialize at work, that's your prerogative—enjoy the flexibility that remote work gives you to spend time with whomever you want.

Household Members Supporting Full-Time Remote Workers

As more people move into remote work, it's really important to have discussions about how to get the support you need from people in your household, particularly if you will be working from home.

You need to have frank discussions about household responsibilities and how you aren't in charge of all of them by default simply because you work from home. You also need to communicate to everyone under your roof what you need to get your work done, such as preserving certain hours of the day for quiet time. Your job isn't any less important just because you can do it from anywhere, and everyone who shares space with you needs to respect that.

Shifting Focus from Hours to Outcomes

Prioritize the work and the output, not the hours. That's the attitude organizations must take to thrive in a future where remote work is common. It's a tenet of the remote-first approach.

Focusing on outcomes or output gives you, the worker, much more flexibility to live your life how you want and get work done when it's best for you.

Communicating Goals and Objectives

Shifting the focus to outcomes instead of hours also pushes everyone in a business to think more about goals and objectives. After all, at work you're meant to be achieving something. Being clear about that is good for everyone. It pushes the organization to communicate its long-term goals.

It also nudges the business into being clear about what you're expected to do in your role and by when, which, historically, a good deal of employers in the knowledge work sector have not been great at. It's really a win-win situation.

Maintaining Balance, Preventing Burnout

A side effect of clarifying and communicating goals and outcomes is being clear about the organization's long-term vision. When a business can explain to you what its ultimate vision is, it gives you additional perspective on how your work contributes to it.

Additionally, knowing the long game and being able to talk about it is good for you. It allows you to develop the mentality of work being a marathon rather than a sprint, which is a useful frame of mind for maintaining work–personal life balance and preventing burnout.

Keeping Touch with the Human Side

In the remote-work future, you're not solely responsible for preventing your own burnout. The organization needs to be cognizant of it as well. Your manager and the organizational culture at large need to be emotionally aware in the sense that employees are treated as individuals with a variety of needs to feel fulfilled and happy in life. In remote work, where people rarely see each other face-to-face, that takes a little more effort.

Some all-remote organizations have been successful at seeing employees as individuals and giving them what they need by offering unique perks, such as paid sabbaticals and stipends for learning or personal enrichment. It also comes through in remote work culture, based on how managers express their appreciation and how coworkers interact to show empathy and encouragement for one another.

Making the Most of In-Person Time

A future with more remote work means the amount of in-person time you spend with colleagues and clients will be significantly reduced compared to what it was at in-person workplaces. Because time together will happen less often, you'll learn to make the most of it and better understand the value of in-person time.

Or at least that's the ideal. Changing something as deeply rooted as working with other people in the same place won't be easy, and it won't happen overnight. The more people are aware of remote work and how it's done best, and the more they design businesses for remote work, the more likely this fundamental change will start to happen, however slowly.

Fewer Meetings, More Focus and Intention

Meetings will take place less frequently as more people learn and develop skills for collaborating asynchronously. More people will understand what a meeting can accomplish that can't be done as well or as effectively by other means, including making decisions quickly, reading people's emotional responses, and getting to know one another better.

Of course, there won't be zero meetings, and the amount of time you spend in meetings could still feel like it's more than is strictly necessary.

It will be hard for some professionals, especially those whose prior experiences took place in the physical world, to shake the belief that frequent meetings and face-to-face contact aren't always the best way to reach the desired outcome. It's going to be a major shift for business culture generally speaking.

People who are knowledgeable and experienced in the ways of remote work will have to be the leaders of change when it comes to reducing meetings in particular.

The Role of Retreats

The rise of remote work will lead to more work retreats, probably annually or twice annually, depending on the size of the organization and what other business travel is in store for employees. If you started working remotely only after the COVID-19 pandemic, there's a chance you haven't experienced retreats yet. Your employer may not have considered them yet. But if your organization is going to have a significant remote work component in the long run, rest assured retreats or other annual or twice annual gatherings will become a part of how business gets done.

Organizations can learn a lot by looking at how some of the trailblazing all-remote companies have used retreats and occasional in-person meetings to keep up certain parts of their businesses. Retreats give people that rare in-person time to bond and learn more about one another, as well as get in-person training. Retreats are also valuable for stepping back and thinking differently about work for a few days because everyone has a longer stretch of time to brainstorm and discuss ideas.

Retreats are also a unique opportunity for you to check in with founders, managers, and leaders in a different way that can give you more insight into the bigger picture of the future of the organization.

In-Person Time Within a Hybrid Setup

It's hard to say what the future will hold for in-person time at organizations that adopt a hybrid model because no one knows yet how hybrid businesses will look. There's a definition for hybrid workplaces, and there are options for how it can play out, but no one yet knows what the experience will be like for either employees or business managers after several months and years of operating that way.

Perhaps some hybrid workplaces will hold in-person, all-hands meetings once a quarter or twice yearly in lieu of a weeklong retreat. Or they might coordinate people's schedules so that all team members work together in-person a certain number of days out of every month. It's hard to say since so little is known at this stage about what hybrid workplaces will be and how workers will feel about them. If you're in a hybrid workplace, be sure to be vocal about what you want and why. You're in a position to have influence.

Make Change from the Bottom Up

Since the onset of the COVID-19 pandemic, so many organizations have started down the path of including remote work as part of their business without learning how to do it right or planning for it. Remote work remains poorly defined and poorly managed in many organizations. The silver lining to this dark cloud is that you have a unique opportunity to steer conversations about remote work, influencing the policies, practices, and culture around it. You can effect change.

Case Study: Change from the Bottom Up

At Help Scout, employees have had significant say in how the company operates, including how much people get paid. When Nick Francis, CEO and cofounder of Help Scout, started his remote organization, he and his team didn't have any formal way of addressing issues of diversity, equity, and inclusion (DEI). The company, which has employees in eighty cities around the world, has a strategy now, but Francis says it wasn't his doing.

"I would love to say that the DEI strategy was a top-down effort, that we were doing it the whole time, but it was bottom-up," Francis says. "This is what our employees demanded that we do well and that we commit to and continue to work on."

DEI takes many shapes and forms, from how the company hires to the standards it holds people to across the organization. In a remote organization, where employees may be located all over the world, it also comes into play with compensation. For example, Help Scout employees in the US and

Canada, where the company has subsidiaries, receive benefits that have a financial value, such as a retirement plan. But workers in other countries don't qualify for them, so Help Scout addressed the gap in compensation by giving those employees an additional stipend to make up the difference.

This example just goes to show that workers can have real influence in how a business is run.

Share Your Feedback

One of the ways to have influence in a remote company is to share your feedback. When you've been with a team or organization long enough to know what works and what doesn't, and, crucially, why those insights matter, you need to talk to your coworkers and managers about what you've observed and ask if they agree.

Practice by sharing positive feedback. It's a way to exercise your feedback muscles and improve at noticing what's going well within your team or related to your work.

Participate in Remote Work Culture

Another way to effect change is through participating in remote work culture. What kind of organization do you want to work at? Aside from creating groups and clubs to socialize, you can also pull together people who share similar views as you about how the organization can run better, and then you can present those ideas to managers and leadership with one unified voice.

Don't forget about the small ways you can participate in remote work culture too. When you're having a good day, be a positive force for other people who might need a boost. Share good news. Ask people how they're doing. Encourage your peers to take breaks when they need them.

In remote work, it takes a little extra effort and thought to do these little actions that can have big effects. Make a point of doing this.

Spread What You Know and Your Experiences about Remote Work

Now that you know all about how remote work works, you can share what you've learned with others and try it out for yourself. Working remotely is different for everyone, depending on your job, circumstances, personality, and many other factors.

Being exposed to a range of ideas can help you find tips and tricks you might not have ever considered before, but you don't always know what's best until you try them out firsthand. Be open to trying new things, and remember that you can change your mind and make adjustments at any time. Talk to your friends and colleagues about what you've tried and what has worked or hasn't worked. Most people are continually figuring out what works for them. Be a part of that learning and sharing process to make remote work better for everyone.

APPENDIX A

REFERENCES

Alexander, Andrea et al. "What Employees Are Saying about the Future of Remote Work." McKinsey & Company, 1 April 2021. https://mckinsey.com/business-functions/organization/our-insights/what-employees-are-saying-about-the-future-of-remote-work.

Al Horr, Yousef et al. "Occupant Productivity and Office Indoor Environment Quality: A Review of the Literature." *Building and Environment* vol. 105 (August 2016): 369–89. https://doi.org10.1016/j.buildenv.2016.06.001.

Bloom, Nicholas. "To Raise Productivity, Let More Employees Work from Home." *Harvard Business Review*, January–February 2014. hbr.org/2014/01/to-raise-productivity-let-more-employees-work-from-home.

Bloom, Nicholas et al. "Does Working from Home Work? Evidence from a Chinese Experiment." *The Quarterly Journal of Economics* vol. 130, no. 1 (February 2015): 165–218. https://doi.org/10.1093/qje/qju032.

Coker, Brent L.S. "Freedom to Surf: The Positive Effects of Workplace Internet Leisure Browsing." *New Technology, Work and Employment* vol. 26, no. 3 (21 October 2011): 238–47. https://doi.org/10.1111/j.1468-005x.2011.00272.x.

"Commuting and Personal Well-Being, 2014." Office for National Statistics, 12 February 2014. webarchive.nationalarchives.gov.uk/20160131203938/www.ons.gov.uk/ons/rel/wellbeing/measuring-national-well-being/commuting-and-personal-well-being--2014/art-commuting-and-personal-well-being.html#tab-5--How-important-is-actual-commuting-time-.

Cornell University Ergonomics Web. "Ergonomic Guidelines for Arranging a Computer Workstation—10 Steps for Users." Accessed 13 May 2021. https://ergo.human.cornell.edu/ergoguide.html.

Cornell University Ergonomics Web. "Sitting and Standing at Work." Accessed 13 May 2021. https://ergo.human.cornell.edu/CUESitStand.html.

Cross, Rob et al. "Collaborative Overload." *Harvard Business Review*, January–February 2016. hbr.org/2016/01/collaborative-overload.

Cullinan, Renee. "In Collaborative Work Cultures, Women Carry More of the Weight." *Harvard Business Review*, 24 July 2018. hbr.org/2018/07/in-collaborative-work-cultures-women-carry-more-of-the-weight.

Elsbach, Kimberly, and Daniel Cable. "Why Showing Your Face at Work Matters." *MIT Sloan Management Review*, Summer 2012. https://sloanreview.mit.edu/article/why-showing-your-face-at-work-matters/.

Eschleman, Kevin J. et al. "Benefiting from Creative Activity: The Positive Relationships Between Creative Activity, Recovery Experiences, and Performance-Related Outcomes." *Journal of Occupational and Organizational Psychology* vol. 87, no. 3 (17 April 2014): 579–98. https://doi.org/10.1111/joop.12064.

Gajendran, Ravi S., and David A. Harrison. "The Good, the Bad, and the Unknown about

Telecommuting: Meta-Analysis of Psychological Mediators and Individual Consequences." *Journal of Applied Psychology* vol. 92, no. 6 (2007): 1,524–41. https://doi.org/10.1037/0021-9010.92.6.1524.

Granovetter, Mark S. "The Strength of Weak Ties," *American Journal of Sociology* vol. 78, no. 6 (May 1973): 1,360–80. https://doi.org/10.1086/225469.

Konrad, Alex. "Zoom, Zoom, Zoom! The Exclusive Inside Story of the New Billionaire Behind Tech's Hottest IPO." *Forbes*, 31 May 2019. www.forbes.com/sites/alexkonrad/2019/04/19/zoom-zoom-zoom-the-exclusive-inside-story-of-the-new-billionaire-behind-techs-hottest-ipo/.

Koonin, Lisa M. et al. "Trends in the Use of Tele-health During the Emergence of the COVID-19 Pandemic—United States, January–March 2020." *Morbidity and Mortality Weekly Report* vol. 69, no. 43 (30 Oct. 2020): 1,595–99.https://doi.org/10.15585/mmwr.mm6943a3.

MBO Partners. A State of Independence in America Research Brief. "Digital Nomadism: A Rising Trend." 2018. https://s29814.pcdn.co/wp-content/uploads/2019/02/StateofIndependence-Research-Brief-DigitalNomads.pdf.

Microsoft. 2021 Work Trend Index: Annual Report. "The Next Great Disruption Is Hybrid Work—Are We Ready?" 22 March 2021. https://ms-worklab.azureedge.net/files/reports/hybridWork/pdf/2021_Microsoft_WTI_Report_March.pdf.

The Nielsen Company. "The Nielsen Total Audience Report, Special Work from Home Edition." August 2020. www.nielsen.com/wp-content/uploads/sites/3/2020/08/nielsen-total-audience-report-aug-2020.pdf.

Parker, Kim et al. "How the Coronavirus Outbreak Has—and Hasn't—Changed the Way Americans Work." Pew Research Center, 9 December 2020. www.pewresearch.org/social-trends/wp-content/uploads/sites/3/2020/12/PSDT_12.09.20_covid.work_fullreport.pdf.

PwC. "It's Time to Reimagine Where and How Work Will Get Done." PwC's US Remote Work Survey. 12 January 2021. www.pwc.com/us/en/library/covid-19/us-remote-work-survey.html.

Roenneberg, Till. *Internal Time: Chronotypes, Social Jet Lag, and Why You're So Tired*. Cambridge: Harvard University Press, 2017.

Statista Research Department. "Leading Distractions among Employees While Working from Home During the Coronavirus Outbreak in the United States As of June 2020." 31 Jul. 2020. www.statista.com/statistics/1139757/us-distractions-while-working-from-home-during-coronavirus/.

US Department of Labor. "Family and Medical Leave Act." Wage and Hour Division. 7 June 2021. www.dol.gov/agencies/whd/fmla.

US Department of State—Bureau of Consular Affairs. "Your Health Abroad." 25 June 2021. www.travel.state.gov/content/travel/en/international-travel/before-you-go/your-health-abroad.html.

GLOSSARY OF TERMS

all-hands meeting

A meeting where everyone in the organization is invited to attend.

asynchronous

Not in real time; usually used to describe communication or collaboration where all parties participate when it is convenient for them rather than at the same time.

broadcast call

A conference call in which one or more parties broadcast themselves to participants, and the participants are typically prohibited from speaking or appearing on video during the broadcast, though they may be able to speak on the call to ask questions at the appropriate time.

capture-and-share

A method of working in which workers are encouraged to keep records of their work and make it available to other employees.

contractor

A worker who is not a direct employee of an organization but is brought on to complete specific work. Contractors do not have the same rights or benefits as full-time employees.

digital nomad

A remote worker who does not permanently live in any one location, usually because they have prioritized traveling as a way of life.

emoji

Small images, symbols, and icons used in text-based writing, often used to convey emotion or state of mind succinctly.

ergonomics

The applied science of designing and arranging objects so that people can use them safely and efficiently. In the context of remote work, usually in reference to office furniture and equipment adjusted appropriately to prevent injury while allowing for comfort.

Family and Medical Leave Act

A US law that entitles eligible employees of covered employers to take unpaid leave for specified family and medical reasons, during which time, the employee will not lose their job and group health insurance coverage continues under the same terms and conditions as if the employee had not taken leave. See the US Department of Labor's FMLA page for additional details related to length of coverage and other applicable terms.

flexwork, flexible remote work

Terms referring to when an employee negotiates the option to work remotely part-time either on an ad hoc basis or a fixed schedule, usually with the understanding that the employee works in person at a fixed location the majority of the time.

focus sprint

A methodology for working whereby the worker sets an intention to work with focus on one task, uninterrupted, for a defined period of time, usually less than sixty minutes, followed by a short, timed break of a few minutes.

freelancer

An independent and usually self-employed worker who earns money by completing projects for clients.

globalization, globalized workforce

In the context of remote work, these terms refer to the ability for an employer to have workers who are based in various locations around the world, with different backgrounds, cultures, and values.

hot-desking

A type of workplace setup in which workers do not have a fixed desk or workstation but rather choose any available workspace each day that they come to the job site. The workstations may have a computer terminal where the employee logs in to access their virtual desktop, while in other situations, employees may be required to bring laptops with them.

hybrid

A work arrangement that blends in-person work and remote work. Because the term "hybrid" is somewhat new within the context of remote work, it isn't as concretely defined as it may be in a few years, after organizations have used it for some time.

microbreak

A very short break, generally between a few seconds and about a minute, from working. In the context of seated knowledge work, microbreaks are typically used to prevent physical injury, as the worker moves their body to change their posture or stretch, and move their eyes away from a computer monitor. Microbreaks can also be a short break for the mind and are sometimes Internet-based (the worker may look online for a minute at social media, news, sports scores, etc.).

OKRs

An acronym for "objectives and key results," which is a method for defining, measuring, and aligning goals within an organization, popularized at Google.

one-on-one

A type of recurring meeting between a manager and employee, typically driven by the employee to address work and work-related issues, as well as check in on and discuss the employee's career intentions.

output over hours

A mindset commonly promoted in remote-first organizations that values the output of an employee over the number of hours the employee works.

Pomodoro Technique

A technique for working with focus, coined by Francesco Cirillo, that is similar to focus sprints but uses more precise measurements. According to its original blueprint, a worker (or student) times a twenty-five-minute focus session, followed by a short break of a few minutes, and then the cycle repeats. After four cycles, the worker or student takes a slightly longer break.

reacji

Emoji used to show a reaction to online content, such as a written post.

remote-first

Describing organizations that build their business process and culture around the assumption that employees work remotely. A remote-first approach contrasts with businesses that build first as in-person workplaces and only later adapt how they operate to accommodate remote work issues.

Schedule Send feature

A feature in email and other communication apps that allows you to schedule the time and date that a message will send, as opposed to sending it immediately upon writing it.

screen sharing

The act of sharing the contents of one's computer screen with participants on a video call.

sprint

In the context of remote work, a sprint refers to a scheduled amount of time in which a worker or team of workers makes progress on a task or project. "Focus sprints" generally refer to work done by solo workers in an amount of time measured in minutes. This is not to be confused with other kinds of work sprints, which may refer to a period of time measured in days or weeks done by a team.

standing meeting, stand-up meeting

A recurring meeting meant as a check-in for team members that's usually somewhat short in comparison with other meetings.

synchronous

Simultaneous; in the context of remote work, this term refers to types of communication and collaboration that happen among people in real time. The opposite of "asynchronous."

team messaging app

A software application used by teams to communicate day to day, such as Slack and Microsoft Teams. Team messaging apps are designed to be used either synchronously or asynchronously, and generally they are for internal team members and select third parties (such as long-term contractors) only.

time blocking

The process of scheduling time on one's calendar in advance for specific tasks or work.

town hall

A type of meeting where everyone in the entire organization is invited to attend.

universal power supply

Hardware that delivers power between a wall socket and electronic devices, and which acts as an immediate backup battery when the primary power supply is interrupted, as in the case of a blackout or energy cut.

vCard

A file format for virtual address books, containing a person's complete contact information, such as their professional title, business affiliation, address, phone numbers, and other details.

virtual whiteboarding

A digital version of a whiteboard, generally used for collaboration among remote teams, which can be saved, shared, and searched.

workflow

The steps or sequence required to move work from the beginning to the end of its process.

work management, workflow management software

Applications, usually designed to be used collaboratively by teams, that workers use to write down and track the progress of work through a defined sequence.

INDEX

ABOUT THE AUTHOR

Jill Duffy is a writer, speaker, and journalist covering remote work, personal productivity, and technology. She's a longtime contributing editor and columnist at *PCMag*, where she writes about software, tools, and techniques people can use to stay organized and productive. Her column, "Get Organized," which has been running since 2012, teaches people how to be more organized in their digital lives, regardless of technical skill level. Her work has also appeared on FastCompany.com, *BBC Worklife*, and Reviewed.com, as well as in *Popular Science*, among other print and online publications.

She also speaks at corporate functions, conferences, and educational events about personal productivity, remote work, and technology. Since 2008 she has worked remotely on and off in a variety of configurations, and has been full-time remote since 2015. She brings a global perspective to her writing, having lived and worked in the US, the UK, Romania, India, and Guatemala.